Blood Orange

KABDO

Charleston, SC
www.PalmettoPublishing.com

Blood Orange
Copyright © 2020 by Kabdo
Illustrated by Kabdo

First Edition

Hardcover ISBN: 978-1-64990-503-1

this book is dedicated to the women whom bathed me in rainbows.

mom

grammy

jane

erin

elena

micheala

lizzy

juliet

autumn

kitty

josie

Contents

1. a girl moves to the city

/these words that I write,
are all that I have left in me,
so I stored them on these pages for you
and after sorting through
you can decide
of what to make in all of this cluttered chaos\

/I've had many different people in my life ask me
how I became to think in the way that I do
of whom hurt me to this extent
for me to become *this* cynical
speaking like a politician
speaking on how they'll save me from these other men
how they lie
how they say they don't partake in this same shame
you claim to want to save me
but you don't want to listen
when I tell you that this is who I am
it is engrained in me
to think in the way that I do
to feel this
to be this
because,
I am the wolf,
and I am the fox,
this is second nature to me
it is who I am
if I need saving
I will save myself
I am no damsel in distress\

run boy run–

/*if I could just write him into poetry…*
and I did
and I did
scribbled out these fine delicate lines of lost love
to get this out of my disarranged mind
because I cannot find the courage to speak these words out loud
so smothered ink into his name
to be rid of him
that's what I'll do,
I said,
I'll kill him off as poetry…\

the girl with the violet eyes–

/aged strawberry rolling paper
I can still smell that taste
she looks at me with the joint between her fingers,
lets get away,
static of the Rolling Stones plays
rolling stoned through this melancholy avenue
got us feeling smooth
like we used to
on these wavy nights
out in my old stomping ground

wondering how I managed to get out
though she stuck around
these thoughts continue to linger on my mind
now that I moved to Chi town
steady smoking sativa
with sticky stained highs
and her Guess low rise jeans complimented her violet eyes
though I asked for the cosmos to take them back to their skies
how they needed her color
as I needed her advice
but she's too stubborn to listen
while I pled my case
to a closed minded judge
as these doobie ashes drift away,
don't take this from me,
and that same stretch of river she meets me at
it still runs through my veins
but she's told me of how I lost my blood
lost these twin cities
and lost her
when I moved away\

/even though you have left this place
it still can haunt you
it is who you are
these 18 years,
you can't run away from what you've been through,
she says to me
as it takes time to sink in\

4

the roommate-

/I looked around this room
this was supposed to be my new space
more like a walk-in closet
shared with a girl
who sang Disney classics
to the top of her lungs
and what aggravated me most
was how she decorated our closet to the tone of a bible camp,
     glitter fest
the last time I went to bible camp
I was in 6th grade
I loathed it so much that I told all the girls in my cabin I was a
     lesbian
because they told us that God hated lesbians
I was mostly straight
I just wanted to give them a little conflict
something to talk about
I barely wanted to be in this tiny apartment
especially with a girl who's driver license claimed she was of age
but her clip-in-plastic bows said other whys
I knew no one in this city
and no one knew me
Chicago immediately threw a knife at my size six-and-a-half-feet
and shouted at me,
Minnesota nice, learn how to speak
learn how to fight back
or die in silence,

and I said,
… alright
toss me that knife

/I couldn't sleep
most nights
turned my pillow over so many times
it never got cold on one side
and my roommate insisted on listening to *Alvin and The Chipmunk's*
    reruns
to go to bed at night
and I remembered how my mom said,
once you leave home,
coming back
it won't ever feel like the same home again

/but as far as I was concerned this wasn't my home
and back home wasn't my home
and my roommate was nowhere near my family
and my family was nowhere near this city
and that emptiness
sunk in deep
I had never felt so empty

so out of body
and I had never craved human connection
more than I did in those times of silence
I prayed for a connection
for any true connection amongst this chaotic city\

then, I met him–

/I could correctly say that I was buzzed off barcardi
he was browned out from Dos Equis
the first time we met
we shared a taxi home from that frat party
I remember he rambled on and on
hyper like a dog who's owner just got home from a nine to five
the whole twenty minute car ride was him yammering
with my subtle *ah's* and *nods*
I followed him through the jungle of his stories
I surprisingly agreed with everything he said about life and his
    theories
he talked until we got to our apartments
stumbling up the stairs with stories
living across the hall from each other
he stopped at his door, while I unlocked mine
his caramel brown eyes stared me down
as he said to me,
you know,

he pointed his unsteady finger my way,
you're easy to talk to,
I grinned at the look plastered onto his drunken face,
I don't usually do that…
he murmured almost only to himself
you don't usually drink this much?
I laughed
*no, I mean, no, I don't usually get this drunk, but I mean I don't talk like
    that to people,*
as he thought for a moment,
I like talking to you, though,
I nodded to let him go on
you… you know, you actually listen
most people these days
they have no clue how to actually listen to 'nother person
and you listen
so thank you… you know, for listening to me

/I remember we would always walk to the harbor
he mentioned vaguely of not knowing his father
but wouldn't go near the subject of a dad any further,
he told me when he was a child he had a sail boat
his dad would take him out there on Lake Michigan every Sunday
    morning,
he used to tell me this was the ocean,
as he scanned his whole arm across the skyline of the water,

because I think to him the ocean was more important
you know, better than a lake
he had me thinking for years that this was the ocean,
he said confidently,
that I was brave,
because I could sail above the sharks and the big waves
and that everyone else who wasn't us envied us,
I would get into fights with my middle school teacher
saying you know, 'you're wrong, this is the ocean',
cause my dad said this was the ocean so there wasn't a doubt in my mind
I remember how he paused for a moment trying to focus on
    changing the subject from his absent father,
it's funny to think when you're a kid you just automatically assume your
    parents are always right
everything they say, everything they do, everything they teach you
it has to be true
then, you get older
and realize… they aren't always right

/it's as if God had painted his soul yellow
I saw so clearly
that he was yellow in my eyes
and I knew that my soul was already stained violet
though instantly drawn to him
unlike any other
his energy I envied

but what I came to realize
how he held within himself
an indecisive mind
while my mind had been decided
and there I sat, as I let his heart mix in with mine
bleeding yellow into violet
a combination of a different color
I would've never before intended
to let a heart blend in with my own
blood orange

/he was different from most of these boys in this city
he was humble
all these other boys whined for attention
most of them just wanted to gain something from you
he was genuine\

/to find a human who you really need to take the time to know
to understand some of their story
a bit of their character
to wait patiently to hear of that reveal
is so satisfying
it is much more beautiful that way\

/because he had me believing in this
when I did not expect to believe in this\

/he was like warm conversation
after a long day of working
for that modelo in my hand
as we sat on the ledge
of that old, echoing lighthouse
the same place we would always go
to watch the waves tumble over the melting sun
wishing we could one day stand beyond these shorelines
until the water ran calm
and the sun said goodnight
the air grew quiet
while the world told me
how I could finally be at peace with myself
a whole new beginning\

/my dad gave away his prized possessions when I left the twin
    cities
old records of which he kept safety hidden
since the age of his childhood lessened
and decided to give them to his only daughter
who's spirit was sworn to be birthed in the 70's
the relationship with my father was mostly communicated through
    old music

long drives
walks around the river
discussing worldly subjects or funny stories
what I realized in those times with my father
those were the safe spaces
I would find myself years from now still walking down to that river
with him there
even if he did not say much
I always knew he was there
though I don't think he recognized how much this meant to me
I didn't seem to realize until I left the twin cities
as I thumbed through those old, coffee stained
album covers
crossing over the pencil scribbles of the little marks he wrote on
    there as a child
I would play them on my record player when I felt so empty in this
    temporary apartment
letting the sound carry me away
while I found myself missing my dad more and more each day
how I would wake up in the mornings and hear him playing
a Dylan song on his guitar
would've given the records back just to have him walk with me
    down to the new harbor or drive me through this unfamiliar
    city
through attempting to avoid nostalgia
I knocked on my neighbors door
my only friend in this metropolis
and I took him to my living room
as I let Led Zeppelin spin

waited for the song to smash
for my favorite part to play
when it did
I looked at his caramel brown eyes
asking if it made him feel some type of way\

/there is no lie to it,
every person around him is ignited from the fire that is his spirit\

/spending time with him
was like coming back home\

/as we rode bikes around the city at night
I remember how he told me that he liked me
it created butterflies floating around in the pit of my stomach
as I was reluctant to let them fly out
I kept them locked inside
I regretted not reciprocating the affection\

/he would speak to me on nights
where I did not want another word brush past my ear
but somehow
after moments of him speaking to me
I'd forgotten
that I wanted to hear someone again\
/he was my neighbor
my first friend
the one whom I trusted
blood orange doused within him
till the moon falls asleep again
he was home to me\

natural instincts-

/I remember when he asked me,
at what point did you get these trust issues?
and I said to him,
at what point did the fox decide she could no longer trust the wolf?

2. a girls truth comes out

beginnings of this–

/he whispers to me
a year later that he is in love
but I will never allow myself to breathe those words
back because how could this be love?
tell me how this is love when we can't let
anybody else
hear us say
this is love

/I suppose, I kept him in good company
while she was living out of state\

/don't start making me believe in something that would always be a
fiction fairytale\

/a year later,
I came back to Minnesota
and I drove along the river road
as I did back when I would ditch high school
just to get away for awhile
and I saw them hanging there
those empty wine bottles from that weeping willow
back when we tried desperately to find ourselves

I found myself now
or so I thought
but I've noticed that I am still the same as I was
only grown a little bit more
and learned a whole lot more

I remember those days the most,
I remember those words the most,

I remember the way life tasted back in Minnesota
how it was not nearly the same flavor
as Chicago
and I remember the advice my dad used to give me
it wasn't often that I could corner my dad in an enough vulnerable
    state
to ever project his advice onto me
but it seemed that I could get him to speak more freely here

so when I saw that boy picking at that same willow tree with his
    dad
he reminded me of how I felt as a kid
how I asked my father what everything around me meant
not knowing what I would know now
just discovering
quietly
and letting the world take me as I went

this kid,
I saw that we both stared at the same weeping willow
but he did not see it weep the way I saw it
and in his mind no bottles hung from that tree
like they swayed in mine
I knew that he was thinking something horribly dissimilar in con-
    trast to my own thoughts
and I wondered what this kid would realize later on,
as I realized some years later on
what kinds of things he would come to discover
I remember when I allowed the world to influence me

I did miss that
now it seems as though I know what I know
and I don't see anything in unfamiliar shades anymore
I see it
as it is
the only way I can see it
the only way I seem to know how to see it
sometimes I wish that I could see things differently again\

/how can I let go of him?
I would think before I considered letting go of him
he had become my best friend
my neighbor
my fondest memories of moving to this city
seemed to always be consumed with him
lighting up my world with just his laugh
I knew well before
that losing this yellow in my life
would be a tragic loss\

/and my best friends would tell me,
Carmen, you can't fall for him anymore
I found myself instantly defending us

coming up with anything to convince them that what we were
    doing would work out
when the entire time
I was trying desperately to convince myself
because I knew it would never work out\

/she was the type of girl you'd rather watch on mute\

/and he fucked me good finally
the first time
waited so long
like nobody else could
road him down
like the Arabian horse that I was
towards that burning sun
and I'll bring him that horizon
each time that he cums
loved the way I held his wrists down
while he smirked at me
like he hadn't felt this good since his mom's homemade spaghetti
as I took him through those rose painted petal clouds
and we shared each other's rhythm
seeing how I bloomed purple violets between my thighs whenever I
    was near him

how the story would climax
lay my head down on his one pillow twin bed
roll that blunt for us later to split
and I can ride him all over again
until the sun sets
but I'll sip on my thoughts until then\

/funny
how he told me
that he was no gambling man\

/I remember the first time
I tripped in this city
sitting in the backyard of our apartment complex
with my close friends
listening to radio head on Margo's speaker set
we painted the stars on the palms of her hands
and I was in a whirl wind
of a whimsical daze
feeling like a true hippie in my element of this aged, blue city
seeing the skyscrapers touch the moons face
and then as it all fell straight
the flowers I gave to the sky

scattered out the city's name
dripping down the backs of buildings
like a drag queens golden hair extensions
as she saunters through taxi cabs
and as I painted pink on my somewhat blank canvas
I looked up and saw him
I remember how I felt this electric shock of blissfully happiness
as he crouched down next to my canvas
I didn't know how to articulate this on acid
though I attempted in the best way an artist could
I painted a violet on his arm
and told him that was my symbol of love for him
and then I asked for him to leave
because that was all the love I could allow myself to breathe\

/and I suppose…
she must've known
girls always seem to know these things
I was just so good at pretending
and she was so good at pretending
pretending to be blinded by the fact
that we had both fallen for the same man\

/I did…
I fell so in love with his soul
captivated in his riveting character
and eventually
I became very conflicted
and it broke me somewhat
to see a soul like that
become so toxic\

/it was a year of my life
and somehow I couldn't give up
he was my best friend
and I believed in him
I've never believed in these sorts of things
even so,
I saw blood orange
I am not proud of what I've done
I loathed him and myself
for how we let this idea of sex and love
poison the both of us\

/it is hard to talk of
how I remember each time I saw her
I would watch as she showed him love

envious at her freedom to be frivolous with her love to him
but while he was mine,
but while he was hers,
and while I wanted to mule over that word she had used to de-
    scribe them
I could not but feel hate instead
when I saw her with him
I forced myself to pretend
and I hated how I forced myself to pretend
pretending that I am not apart of this
pretending that she is not apart of this
pretending that he is not apart of her
as I watched them together
I turned away
before my eyes could catch up to my suffocating heart
she is not his entirely,
I would say this often to myself
as the girl with the violet eyes came to me
whispering in my ear,
do not look away,
you cannot shield your eyes from your part in this adultery,
but I chose to close them anyhow
lying to myself
that the next time I would open my brown eyes
this scene of her and him
I would never have to see again\

/oh,
well it must've slipped my mind
of how it was like breathing in nicotine
every time I let him kiss me again\

/he says that he is listening…
but he does not hear a god damned word that I am saying\

/*maybe you only think you need him, because you have no one else to
need,*
I would often try to manipulate my mind
into thinking that I had not truly fallen for him
I have never loved someone before
how do I know what real love is, if I've never loved before
I am not in any rush to be desperate enough to cling onto false love
I know that I do
it has to be
I know that I love him,
because I have never loved someone before\

/using these pretty words

to mask the fact
that these feelings are not so pretty
only pretty when I don't see her
only pretty when I am with him
and only pretty when I don't allow myself to sink deep into this
    guilt
it is not so pretty
when I think about how ugly
this situation really is\

/you chose to close yourself off from any guy in Minnesota
men who were good for you
you chose to push away
but you chose to open yourself up to him?
what happened to your guarded self worth?
did you leave that in Minnesota too?
the girl with the violet eyes asked,
while I took the L home from work
leaving her thoughts in the back of my mind
while I came home
and knocked on his door\

/tell me you want me, and I am yours,
he would say to me
why must I tell you these things

to make this hurt
I've let you put onto me
to become easier on you
when I have showed how vulnerable I am
is that not enough?
leave her because this love is no longer living
do not leave her simply because I am now your consolation prize
I will not be that for you,
I said to him
while I walked away that day
I began to see
the yellow in him fading\

/I just hope your heart can adapt,
to what your mind convinced you to settle for,
I told him\

/don't be afraid to speak
so much that's said in the mind is never heard\

not all these boys have grown up-

/you'll find it's very difficult when having an adult conversation with a
  child

/she's very beautiful...
but what else is she?
I have heard them whisper these sorts of saying's my whole life
I felt as though my life began with a hand over my mouth
and a wall between myself and others
I was questioned constantly of my ethnicity
knowing full well that I was a bit different from these milk white
    toasted
blue eyed
and yellow haired school kids
I was not like them
in so much sense of the word I was not like them
I was dark
with curly, black hair and nearly black eyes
I wasn't intelligent like them
(*the way America views intelligence*)
I would sit alone and recite my stories
I had to memorize them to myself because I could not read or
    write
I was called *retarded*
or a *lesbian*
because of my ethnicity because of my disability
no one knew how to teach a dyslexic
no one knew how to console a little loner

and most of them stayed away from the retard,
the girl with the curly, black hair,
the girl they couldn't quiet put their finger on
my whole life I have been told what I cannot do
questioned
asked of who I am
what else do I have to offer
that I cannot be a writer
it's been 18 years of living
and I am still processing how to not let my past continue to haunt
    me\

as this other woman talks shit about the girlfriend-

/I hear her noisy
drunken
sorority girl
doesn't smoke weed
but on a coke diet
Spotify advertisement
voice
ringing in and out of my ears
she talks too much
talking too much but not saying anything authentic
talking too much but I can predict her like a Telenovela
talking too much but conversing only to be heard

because she lacks personality and intrigue
yet, I am a thunderstorm
booming in and out of his ears
which he covers in order to muffle me out when the grey rabbit is
    around
but what I cannot comprehend
is the attraction to both
engaged in a simple minded, grey rabbit
while he fiends for this lone wolf\

/telling myself that they were doing long distance
was still the wrong excuse to cheat\

/out of sight...
so she wasn't on my mind\

/*why don't you see a therapist? You could use some therapy,*
she said to me
over coffee and weed
I told her,
I'm a writer...

most of our therapy consists of words, coffee, pot and tequila
we're all a lil' jaded

/I felt as though
that every time I was with him
I would catch a thrill\

/and I suppose,
I waded through these interminable waters
with the hope that we would come out clean
from this fucked up love
hiding fear of vulnerability
with the utmost fraudulent elegance
of which I could compose within myself\

/we sat out on Rafi's porch alone
and I could see the skyline
illuminating the harvest moon
drunk like we had to be
to let out these feelings

which the both of us knew would inevitably come out
I assumed it would've been sooner than nearly two years later
... what're you doing with this guy? I didn't expect you to go for someone
     like him,
he attempted to say in a lighter judgement
I am trying to move on from you,
was the truth,
but still I could not have been that vulnerable
so I shrugged my shoulders,
I think he's interesting,
I said simply
are you going to start dating this guy?
he asked
you think for two years I enjoyed knowing you were with Ale? Coming
     outside my apartment and seeing you two together? But I've never
     pressed you about it, because I wanted you to figure this out on your
     own, not to blame me for my bias opinion,
I remember I breathed that out
like I had just gotten done with a 12 hour shift and I had the first
     taste of a cigarette
I know... I know, and I'm sorry-
-if you know, and if you're saying sorry, then that means you're apolo-
     gizing for your mistakes and you don't make those mistakes again.
     You've been making that mistake for two years now, your words lost
     their meaning a long time ago
it's not that easy. You make things seem easy, because you know very well
     how to hide your feelings,
he said
and you hid your feelings of me from Ale very fucking well,

I retorted back
what do you want me to say?
say something that's actually real. 'Cause I never know what you want
in the moment or what you want in the long term, I can't read you
I want to break up with her, and I want to be with you… I've said that.
I know I'm weak, I know I'm not strong like you, but it's really hard
to tell someone who really, really loves you, really loves you that you
don't want to be with them… that you want to be with this girl…
who she's always been jealous of… suspicious of… who's also my
neighbor, who's also my best friend, I don't want to see her get hurt
in that way… I don't want to hurt her like that, I just, I don't know
how to do it in the right way
I looked down at my beer,
there is no right way, no matter what, you're both going to get hurt,
but you don't even want to be with me, so why do you keep on–
I shook my head to stop him from speaking,
I already told you, I won't ever be your girlfriend
then why are we still doing this?
he shouted for once
and I said nothing, because I couldn't seem to formulate that an-
swer
so you'll have sex with me for two years–
I cut him off sharply,
you'll have sex with a different woman than your girlfriend for two
years?
he said nothing now
yeah, put that on your tinder bio when she finally leaves you,
I said as I took an ugly gulp of that piss water we young kids called
beer

but instead of walking away or him walking away
we stayed stuck on that porch
the same way we could not seem to wash off the stickiness of this
    affair
not to say another god damned word, expect to sip quietly on our
    beers
because for the first time in two years
we fully acknowledged
out loud
the mess we had both created
and acknowledged the fact that we were so messy and so soaked up
    with such stubborn hearts
that the both of us couldn't seem to be vulnerable enough
to come together
to clean up this mess
that we left festering on and on for two years too long\

/we had dreams
you know
the silent ones
the kind I would wish for over street pennies
but am I allowed to dream?
if these dreams I want aren't morally correct
or socially acceptable
if not I'll hold onto them
still silently

I'll keep quiet
what I hated most
was to be silenced
lock me up in a box
and take me out for your passing time
but I have decided
that I will no longer be used like this\

popeyes verses harolds-

/the girl with the violet eyes knows...
she knows
and I know she knows...

even though I hide myself like a transparent shadow to a bricked
        wall
the sunlight hits me every once and a while
I'm exposed

no matter how hidden I've become
ask me to write a book, and I'd write it about being the other one...

but who is she?
and who the fuck am I?
to treat you this way
and who are you to treat her this way, to treat me this way?

how did it take me this long
why did I stay?
pretending this is not temporary love
I've found myself in the middle of this mess

so tell me, girl with the violet eyes,
have I lost myself amongst these entangled, impenetrable lies?
or have I found myself amongst these hollowed out narrowed out
    lies?

I've become immune to this mindset now
turned on snooze
I have slept away the thoughts of what I am doing
is this right or wrong?
don't let me think too long
I want to linger on this sort of feeling for a little bit
I've grown to like it, some sort of guilty pleasure
this pleasures me somewhat
I have to admit

to hold this heavy power, this certain power I have in my body, in
    my mind
to control
to corrupt these men
make me feel invincible
I've found that this way is the only way I know how to live
I can't let anyone in
can't let what you claimed to be love, I won't let that in

so hand me a light for this cigarette, if you continue to question my
    morals

don't bust my balls just yet, girl with the violet eyes, you know
    nothing at all
you don't know what it is to be the other woman
visionless, soundless, nameless,
the other woman is
it's not easy being nothing
try to test these waters a bit
they'll wash you out whole
before you know what you're breathing in
find yourself to be emotionless
and you'll become a new woman
amongst this cluttered up mess
in a situation you let yourself fall in

the girl with the violet eyes says I'm a cynical soul
that I've sold my soul away…
maybe she's right

but I don't know how to love
and he calls this love
and how could he say those things?
calling this love?
and he asks me why I could not let him in
he says he won't leave his girlfriend till I trust him
but,

I am the other woman.
I am the other woman.

and I don't know how to love
to love him
to love anyone
sometimes I wish I were ignorant
but still, he was the one whom I was sleeping with
and I do feel something for this bastard, I have to admit
and people thought we were together
good for each other
that we fit like Archer and Bob's Burgers
like hot coffee and donuts
you're right,
these are bitter sweet flavors

do you miss your girlfriend, I used to ask him this often
and somehow
I envied her, to have him as hers
or at least
she had the right to scream to the world that she was his
and I could have nothing but a whisper
I wanted to feel that
all of it
and fill that vacant hole inside of me
I let him dig in too deep
left me feeling empty
but here I am still
the other woman

so tell me how to fix this?

girl with the violet eyes,
in this chaotic city, how am I suppose to pretend that this thing I
    am fighting for is real?
or that she's real?
I've allowed myself to fall short in the reality of her
shielding my part in this adultery
I've squashed these persistent ideas like his cigarette butts
like her bud lights she left out on his back porch to rot
to remind me of *her* and *myself*
and what of myself
I have lost

but I won't lie
he's a pretender, pretending like he's different
when they're all the same
and while I look at him, I suddenly see no potential...
I suppose I've been paying for Popeyes expecting to taste Harold's
but I'm not surprised still

and I saw the way she looked at him
I've seen it so many times
she looks at him like no other man was on her mind
and believe me, no other man is on her mind

and I continue to spin
and spin...

I am the other woman.
I am the other woman.

but these men won't notice
they won't let that sink in
they're too busy thinking of me
the girl they don't have yet
my beauty
my eyes
my other specialties...
he loves my body
makes him feel high
doing wrong, this feeling will rise
works against his, to make him feel more alive again
give *him* what *she* doesn't have
making him believe he has the power
now I'll suck the light out of him
though, he isn't quite sure of all of this yet

so I'll seduce him with my unclear intentions
and messy manners
start to fix him up for disaster
he'll become entangled in my sexy, curly hair
but he won't be able to wrap his fingers around it
and you won't find me here for too long
I like to leave them wondering what happened

therefore, these men will not be on my mind, I've decided
not a single thought can settle with me

I can't let that in especially
but I am used to this now
being used like this
being chosen like this
treated like this
feeling like this
they assume there is no other consequence to being the other
    woman

but believe me there is

and he chooses to use a condom with me, like it's his civic duty
protecting himself from further complications...
I'm sure he doesn't use those rubbers with his girlfriend
the one he lays with in the mornings, and lies to at breakfast
remember that?
with Belgium waffles and over sweetened coffee
she calls this love everyday
and I'm there only at nights
when she's finally giving him space
drinking her cocktails, she thinks of him
and meanwhile I'm in his bedroom, while I fuck the shit out of him

but again,

I am the other woman.
I am the other woman.

he tries to hold me down often

when I say I need to leave
he claims that he's different
that he doesn't love her anymore
was a mistaken discussion
to keep her around for so long
he says he likes me better
that he'll leave her by yesterday's dawn
never follows through with his rights, but he does do wrong
that he doesn't know how to let her go
he says he doesn't want to hurt her
so he continues to fuck me and keep me as a secret
he calls me a "secret lover"
tells me I'm worth it
that I mean something
something real
but I don't listen
turn it off for one second, and you become the girlfriend
and I will never be that…

I am the other woman.
I am the other woman.

as if these lines we were lead by to believe that I was the only one
     in the wrong
that I am the hoe in this scenario, and he's just a one mistake kind
     of guy
I am exposed as the snake
the bitch
the fucking mistress

that I fucked up
that I did this
blame me for his decisions
I can take it
paint me red
so I can stand out bolder for these other cheating men
make me want to do wrong again
don't worry
I haven't forgotten it

and I see this like a relapsing movie in my living room…
over and over again
I will say to myself,

I am the other woman.
I am the other woman.

pore me that drink, you cheater, I don't need a chaser
I'll lick it up like these sloppy seconds, and onto my next male
    attraction
feeding off of these cheap boys
but never satisfied in my actions
so I go to my next man
then he goes home to his girlfriend
and I feel it
I feel this all over again
and I say to myself…

why I am the other woman?

why I am the other woman?

so what is it like to be this way?
the girl with the violet eyes keeps asking until I say...
it's knowing the secrets, but not being able to do anything about it,
     because I am all apart of it
I am the secret...
and I am everything
and I am nothing

I am the other woman.
I am the other woman.

the girl with the violet eyes, you know nothing till you are the other
     woman

and then you will know too much
some things you didn't intend on knowing
and this is what I know...
when she finds out of me, he will tell her it was a one time thing
he'll recite her those same fed lines
the same kind he observed those other dirty boys dish out
and leave for their girlfriends to pick at it like their left over cold
     lunch
these are lies that won't ever add up, but she'll take it
she wants to think this was a mistake
but she'll be mistaken
he'll put on the most elaborate show to win her back
even though she's not what he really wants

but she'll believe him, she will pretend to at least, pretend to let it
    go
and she will keep me on her longed, hated mind
blame me with all that she knows

but she knows nothing, she's not the other woman
she is just some other woman

so tell me to write a book again, and I will blow your mind with
    the information I have,
because,

I am the other woman.
I am the other woman.

and I advise that you reconsider the morals of your so called man\

/he could not handle me as a whole
so he had to order me as a side\

/romancing the unrealistic potential of him
was something I should've never fed into my soul\

/cotton candy colors kissed these skylines
the same place you always drove me through back then on those
    nights
look up
you're constantly in a rush
taste these colors before they turn to powder in your mouth

stare a little longer for once
if you don't mind me saying
you're very impatient

these specific areas seemed to have left freckles of marked up mem-
    ories on my blurred out mind
when these were once foreign lands to us
new to our young eyes

but you've ripped into my bones
cut me down deep
and spit me back out
I'll give you a taste of who I am
now can you tell me what you've found?

sideways and nuzzled corners into your neurotic mind
with glowing, yellow lights
I feel it surrounding me now

as you lie awake to think of me
sleeping silently
you silence away what you can't keep

deciding to articulate your speech
attempting to make us sound less complicated
but you're only manipulating your mind from the obvious
with this idea
you think of me
as you hold that other girl
you can't seem to sleep
desperate to feel me
so you touch her
and you let that be the only way you feel something for your other
    girl
you clench the covers
expecting me to hold you through your rough demeanor
in your fucked up position
but no one made you stick to this page
you've left the top corner folded in

I hope she secretly leaves you for another man
so you'll know how it feels
when she's with someone else
though I have no power in all of these plans
to decide what you side with
I cannot change your indecisive
fickle mind
you're the pilot flying this plane
and I'm merely your deadhead on this flight
for the time being\

/if I continue to complain about the same things...
but don't make actions to change anything...
then I remind myself that
the definition of *instantly* is doing the same things over and over
    again
and expecting a different result\

/a few weeks later,
on his birthday,
he left his other woman for *this* other woman
and at that point
it all hit me
as much as I longed to trust him
our entire relationship was built around petrified secrets
hidden feelings
and I told him still,
that I could never be his girlfriend
and I think that hurt him somewhat
though he'd never speak on it
and that's how things ended for us
a few subtle words avoiding the real ones we wanted to say
but still could not speak to each other
still too vulnerable to let ourselves in
he didn't speak to me after that day outside our apartment
I knew I made the right decision
but the pain of losing this lasted longer than my elevated ego when

I refused to stay
I didn't see him again
only heard of him through the grapevine of our entangled friends
eventually he went back to what he knew would be a safe bet
and I went with my safety blanket
alone to myself
while he
stuck back to the grey rabbit
and once again,
I suppose
that we all have our vices\

/the melancholy
the nostalgia
of this forbidden love
was the hardest and yet the easiest to admit
of how this cheater,
I would have equally called him my best friend
I do not have animosity so forth
only some sort of apprehensive lingering sadness
of how I trusted in him
enough to wait for our brokenness
to ultimately subside
but he hurt me most
leaving me alone
to bleed out the darkest shade of violet

while he walked away
glowing yellow
as he held her
while the sun shined on them
as the rain poured on me
for months and months
eventually it ceased
and what grew from the rain I created into fire
I decided to use this red hot violet rage
against these other cheating liars\

3. from being a different girl

/oh, believe me,
that the wrong I had done
all those years ago
I am paying it back
like my fucking student debt\

/she does not come for blood
no, she comes for his heart
how he took hers
left her heartless\

/through these tired blinds of windowed eyes I see so many empty
    people with empty minds
and I see this all the time

and I think about the feeling of feeling something more

but cannot seem to bare to feel again
the over felt feeling of only being intimate with a man
to fill his lost and gaping holes the last woman he loved left him
    with

and they think they're all so slick
coming up with those sweet lines
like he hadn't just smoothed that one over
with his margarine pretending like it's butter the other night
like dripping black honey from a silver spoon
assuming he's fed me up full

to that other woman he sees fit to save him from his loneliness
but unfortunately, she doesn't know it yet

that this is a game these subtle men play to see themselves in a
	better way

because he needs to feel someone to feel something to fill that
	vacant void he let sink in deep
he hides too
too much sometimes he's hard to find
they all seem to now a days
but when I think of running away how can that confront my pain
assuming we need love from another to feed our tempered hearts
	to love the parts of ourselves that we can't seem to love on our
	own terms

but what they don't know, deep inside I side with this
how I allowed another soul to swell up and swallow the bellows of
	my heart and left it to simmer dry
and I say to myself,
what is it to pretend to not love someone who was never mine?

/I feel this
while my heart suffocates in wanting to hate you
with all that I have,
because I need to hate you
so that I do not let myself fill with what I want as love for you
	instead\

/the hardest is to pretend that he did not hurt you\

/I hid behind this fearless mask
which was crafted from my wounded pain
like a sword fighter
who lost her last battle
she decides to go into a one on one combat
against a man who is blind
this sword fighter blindly knows
confident with two eyes
she will come out alive
and win this shallow victory
that seemed to be my tactic
go for the weaker man,
I said,
because these weak men cannot hurt me\

lions and thorns-

/I feel nothing for men anymore, girl with the violet eyes,
they've become too easy
and I seep right into them
like liquified fools gold
while I lie with him on some nights
and lie to him almost every other night
I'll let him believe in those things that he perceives
what he cannot seem to understand
is that I am only an illusion
of someone he wants me to be
but I know exactly where his priorities lie
and they're not genuine anyway
however, I could careless
for meaningless men
as I continue to sleep around with men who mean less
making myself feel not genuine

a cycle I've put myself in
so now I've become inadvertently malicious
and I see that these men envision fire
when I perceive rain
while I light up my joint
and I think
that I'd gladly take his toke
as I could effortlessly take his unintelligible friends
'cause he doesn't know what I know
'cause I know it all too well for him
and I do it better
every
damn
time
I'll leave my lipstick signature on his sweater
every damn time
stained with these warm kisses, but he feels cold
maybe now
he'll catch on more?
and I'll let him slip from my fingers
like a cigarette to a drunk fiend
wrapped up in my phony satin pink bedsheets
I'll go and leave him drowning there
in that mundane mind of his
he knows nothing past
what he cannot see
but this is all just meaningless to me
so he becomes torn…
and what he can't catch onto is

I smell like roses
but I cut like fucking thorns\

/as if these colors were to touch your soul maybe
somehow…
maybe than
you could feel what this all really means\

/I wonder…
how it must feel as good as an orgasm
when a man finally cries…
since they hold that urge back so often
must feel like thunder to the sky\

/I tried to burry myself in writing
writing till my fingers grew numb
letting my numbed out pain
spill onto this burning page
but all that was left in me
was left written about him

and for awhile
writing was an alliance and a vendetta
since it seemed to be poisoned with his name
I needed a new outlet
to hide my pain
so I did what most starving artists do
and I went on searching for new muse\

you catch more flies with honey-

/I remember the look he had
written out
in blotchy black ink
smeared across his dark almond brown eyes
as he laughed at me
with a forlorn scorn
tethered up tight in his raspy voice
dragged out like sharp icicles
a dagger to my throat
as he said to me,
you're like a bee charmer,
taking his gentle eyes
off the gaze of my poison lips
reminding himself out loud,
you can charm anything
even if you don't give a fuck about them

/you don't realize it
until you've realized it for yourself
how heartbreak is petrifying pain
no one should go through that alone
but since he was never mine
and since this was all silenced
and left to silent hurt
I saw tangerine trees growing in and out of my chaotic mind
to pretend that this whole thing never happened
and what was left alive
against the one who broke apart of me
is fueled from this horrible vendetta
leaving me to bleed violet over and over\

/this boy from my art school carried around his guitar like a book
    bag
even when he was drunk at parties
I remember how he asked me once,

what's your aesthetic?
and I replied to him in monotone,
depression and profanity
just to give him a little edge\

/I said,
I pluck pretty flowers
like I pick out pretty boys
but
neither of which
ever lasts that long\

I'll make him fall in love with my mind-

/there is power in a woman
who can entice a man with her body
but if she can seduce a man with her mind
that in its self
is a whole other power\

/running through me
like I'm paper to paradise\

/you're just like everyone else unfortunately...
fiending for someone else's acceptance of your own self worth\

/I said to a man whom I was temporarily seeing,
that's the difference between you and I,
is I know what I want
what kind of man deserves me
and in that I am not afraid of being alone

/he said to me,
I've always liked you,
as I sat there silent
thinking to myself,
I'll like you until I wake up tomorrow morning

/the color of wine flows through my hair
deep dark
reflections of violet
coiled between his fingertips
I swirl around to catch my breath
lets get away for a little while
so I let the mary sit\

she is Athena with that golden armor –

/tell me why I've become so frightened
when I know how strong I am
why do I feel this anxiety
breathless in my entire body
when I realize I am falling for a man

it is as though
I am constantly wearing armor

it glistens even in the darkness
and I admire how I radiate gold
no one can touch this
my interior drips and molds around my body
to hold me together
to protect me against these other sword fighters

while the man who wants me
he stands there naked in the street
but it always starts off like this

I am strong and powerful
he cannot break me,
I have the proper leverage
I have the correct formed body,
I can take him,
if I wanted…
I hold the control
he does not phase me

but then I let my guard down
when I begin to feel something
and as I do
I become more and more naked too

as if each piece of my reliable armor flakes
like shaven gold from my body
it is not an easy task to always protect yourself
to wear this armor
weak people cannot handle this heavy mask

I plead to take this bulging, and dense outerwear off
to feel light again

and now that we stand face to face
I've allowed some pieces of armor to fall off of me

as they fall he picks them up
and straps them onto himself

we seem to be even

though I still have some on
I feel completely naked
and even though he only wears a few of my pieces
I act as though he has taken *my* safety blanket
using *my* armor for only *his* protection

while I am left
stripped whole
from my foraged, golden armor
now the power
is up in the air

though I wish I could just let myself go
I want to be able to sense that happiness I try so hard to suppress
I wish I could be vulnerable
I wish I could let myself love someone
but I can't
I am too stubborn
I am a very calculated well formed mess
don't try teaching this lone wolf
how to love this fox
doesn't seem to work out like that
and that is why
I always keep one dagger

strapped to the back of my hip\

slumdog millionaire-

/the goal is
to eventually be as happy as that dog over there
the one sticking her head outside that car window
I wanna be as freely happy as her\

convertible blues-

/and right after
he sighed
looked me in my eyes and said,
well, the thing is I do have a girlfriend,
as easy as your instincts are when you see a rattle snake
I lifted myself from his chest and walked away
I locked myself in my friends bathroom
immediately I felt that same pain you get as a child
when you take a soccer ball straight to your stomach
I sat down from this excruciating pain
which had already radiated throughout my body
I began to cry
in the most loudest silence I allowed myself to have

I remember seeing myself in that mirror
fog began to coat around this old, unwanted face
something which I was incredibly ashamed to see myself wear
yet again
it was certainly not the first time I had seen it
and it was not the last time
but this was not the story I wanted from him
I told myself instantly,
don't feel, Carmen
don't feel this
do not feel anything for him
as if I rehearsed this bathroom scene 10 times till perfect
I walked out of that bathroom
and found the snake
still sunbathing on the couch where I last left him
let's go,
I said impatient
he got in my convertible, as I drove him back home
don't feel anything
don't let him know you felt something
he tried reasoning with me
as to why he was a cheater
I put his radio static speech on silence
I've heard those memorized lines enough
but I did not act on my angered emotions
I did not act regretful
or sickened by him
I acted like I didn't care
like I didn't care for him

or for her
or for myself
even though I had been seeing him for three months
and none of his friends or my friends ever told me he had a girl-
    friend
he could lie to me for three months
and my friends could lie for him for three months
fuck them
I thought fuming,
fuck him
and fuck myself
I never slept with him again or talked to him again
but a week later, I did sleep with his best friend
funny
how sex got me into this mess
and how I used sex to get revenge
I was still learning…
and yet,
I knew *exactly*
how to make a cheating man tick\

how to find a man without a girlfriend–

/I had asked the girl with the violet eyes
if I had been cursed in some way
she would nod

as if it went without saying
and I do
I still believe
that I am cursed in some way\

/it makes me sad
for people who do not have anything to be passionate about
without my passion
I would be nothing more than a pretty girl
who is only living day by day\

/writing twists my stomach inside out
fills my caged heart with indigo butterflies
leaves me with a better high
writing has been my most intimate relationship
more than any man I have ever slept with
and that's real proof of passion
at 19
I'd pick writing over sex\

because I fear being vulnerable-

/there are so many questions that I have
ones I've been waiting years to be answered
and I know in my heart
that these unanswered questions
I won't ever ask\

/if ever there was a way to take on my friend's pain
I would
my true friends have been my army
and I am their sell sword
I would never stop fighting for my friends\

Graveyard of my vulnerability-

/a long time ago
my faith was buried somewhere in Minnesota...
don't ask me to dig it back up for you\

/you can always trust a cynic
they're too stubborn to switch up on you about who they really are
for the rest of these humans...

you can't trust them
they flip flop too easy\

/too stubborn to see
that I am letting myself drown
drowning in my own self poison
burning up in my own seething passion
drowning in my own rain
too ignorant to see that there is a sun out here\

/I told a friend
whom I truly cared about
that I did not want him in my life anymore
I suppose, I had been the other woman enough
that maybe
by now
this distinct and awful smell
lingered on me
like a smokers jean jacket
I've tried many times
washing my soul clean from it
the fragrance never diminished
entirely

I wondered at what point
would my demons quit tormenting me
when could I be freed from their clawed forces
when would girls stop seeing me as another mistress
I am not her,
anymore,
I tried to promise
I was stuck in hearing awful thoughts she had of me
but for once they were not true
I felt as though her harsh words were combined rambles from all
    the other women that I had hurt
but still
I said goodbye to him
I got so talented at hiding these feelings, that you wouldn't ever
    catch me wearing them
I was learning now
of how these scars still remain visible on my bare skin too
I was terrified of many things
I wanted to be rid completely of my other identity
and I was afraid that my friend would turn to what all the rest of
    the men were doing
and then, I would be tempted to go back to my bad habits
and wear that same label she had already tapped to my face
and then I'd be responsible
in turning my friend into the same man
the kind I was so used to sleeping with
I had no more strength
to defend myself against yet another girlfriend
I chose to say goodbye to him

I became so talented at saying goodbye
that it almost scared me
to be this emotionless
I told a friend
whom I truly cared about
that I did not want him in my life anymore
when saying goodbye to him
I felt absolutely nothing
only a sense of impatience
just to be done with it\

9. the girl and the musician

fear of yellow–

/the hardest part of getting over someone
is getting over someone
the fear of seeing him again
mine was a constant paranoia

that every time I'd walk out my front door
what if I saw him…
what if I saw him with her
six months of silence
six months of hiding
six months of only myself counseling myself to get through this
    hurt
six months of moving on\

/to say that I was using him?
maybe at first
to distract myself of seeing yellow
I wanted to envision a different color
and without recognizing the absence of feeling another
I latched onto him
quicker than normal
the lone wolf still alone
but for a time I followed
and I regret that I was lost
and I regret that I chose to follow the first man who was lost too
I suppose that we both did not know yet
how to want to be found\

/I was long drawn out from being the other woman
that I did not know what it was like
to be a girlfriend
though I promised myself I'd never be the two
I was attempting to better myself
and I fell into the lamp of a starving sad artist
as I was an in denial sad hungry artist myself
it seemed only fitting
that this would turn to be a catastrophic disaster
but in a bloody and gory artistic master piece\

/I really didn't like his friends
the types who refused to shop anywhere besides *Salvation Army*
speaking out about being different
smoking cigs with cliche tattooed hands
and drinking out of PBR cans
for the look of it
not that they enjoyed the taste
and they couldn't understand a girl like me
because I was different
but they could not find a label to match me
they only knew I wasn't their brand name
pretending to be so real
but I saw through their facade
and I knew these were not the people I wanted to be around\

/after dating the musician for a few months
I ran into my neighbor for the first time while carrying my groceries
he was excited to see me
since we never ended things officially
we became friends again slowly
but only friends
I saw him a few times here and there
and I realized how much I missed him
missed his roommates
how I missed that I could wear my sweatpants
drink tequila
and be myself
without any judgement
without being asked of who I was
why I didn't have tattoos
or what art I had produced
I was tired of his friends picking at me
deciding where I fit in their minds\

/although
I'd usually agree you cannot be friends with your ex
but he was never my ex...
and for some reason
us being friends seemed to work\

/being a lone wolf
it is hard to commit
I always wanted to be free\

this is about the musician-

/it's difficult
when attempting to correctly articulate a person
whom you used to care for
scribbling down those moments
you know, the kind that left you feeling so electric
beaming in your hearts eye
when he used to bundle your soul up
fill you to the brim
like no other man could before him
but how to write these down now
when so much of me has changed since then
so much of me was broken from him
the warmth that I remember getting
is no longer fire
it's lathered in ice now
so why does it seem to be
how every time in a relationship
it's a quicker process to put out these kinds of burning fires
than it is to melt these five layered ice sculptures
and I can't seem to find

any sort of words
to articulate him as a good man
when I envision ice colliding into fire
every fucking time
I try to write about him\

/after a few weeks
I saw the neighbor again
said he missed me

what did he miss?
the way I climbed up his ladder of broken intimacy
of these hidden secrets
that I kept hidden for his sake
was he missing how I taste?
how I licked his body to a seemingly clean slate
or does he miss the way he swallowed my intimate words whole
and used them as a blanket to keep him warm

or does he miss how my language sounds
how it oscillates
rolling off my tongue
and back onto his
while he was inside of me
or does he miss the way we were there for each other?
even when he should not have been the one beside me

but like the sun to moon
I was his
and I was there
even when he could not touch me
or hold me down
like he wanted to
but like the sun to the lone wolf
maybe he only missed traits of myself?
perhaps only at night?
or does he miss my stories?
or our friendship?
maybe he does not miss these things at all
maybe he misses the way I left him feeling
after I fucked him raw
because it seemed
she
only left him with a belly full of salad
what he should have
but not what he craves
as I filled him whole
left him every time
with a filet mignon
but now
I was
well done
so it didn't matter anymore
but still I wondered

what is it then?

he must've realized
how he had lost me
he knows now
for certain
what I knew since before this mess really started
that I was the person his heart ached for
I was the person his heart sang thunder for
I was
his
person
but instead he chose to stay with a girl
that kept his heart content
a girl that his mind chose to settle for
while at the same time
he was fucking with the best\

/my roommates ended up giving our whole apartment bed bugs
so I asked my boyfriend if I could sleep at his house
that I would take a shower
wash all my clothes
and his reply was,
my bed is too small
he was worried about his lack of sleep instead of mine
so I continued to toss and turn night after night
smoking so much mary jane just to get some shut-eye
nothing worked

and the god damn exterminator could not come for an entire week
I was so sleep deprived I walked across the hall and knocked on his
    door
and asked if I could spend the night
knowing I had bed bugs he offered up his bed
and he took the couch
in the morning him and his roommates made me black coffee and
    their version of the best grilled cheese
I sat in his pajamas while we played mario cart until 3
I did this for two weeks until the bed bugs were completely gone
and I was reminded why I loved this kid\

/isn't it funny
how we can spend long amounts of time in situations or in places
    we know in our hearts that we
no longer want to be in
and yet for some reason
it seems it's not enough of an incentive
to try and leave the place or the situation
or to leave the person that we no longer want to be with\

/when you know it's not right
but you linger anyways\

/*I think he wants to be with you,*
the musician told me one night,
with his dark eyebrow raised
his thick, black, curly hair coiled between my fingers,
just be careful,
he uttered
but as much as I concentrated on manipulating my mind that the
    musician and I were good for each other
it never felt authentic
I've learned in order to make something work
the both of you need to make sacrifices
majority of relationships are learning how to grow with another
    person
considering the fact that most young people don't even know how
    to properly grow within only themselves
and considering the musician didn't know how to put down his
    damn guitar
and hear me out
to listen to me for only just a moment
if there's only one of us making the sacrifices
that is not a healthy relationship
and I regret how I neglected my own intuition
even when it was screaming in my ear begging me to leave this
    bastard
I was so busy making excuses for his lack of effort
that I began to neglect my own self
in that matter
because I was so consumed
wrapped up in making him happy

the cosmos couldn't catch me
I flew off lightyears away from my own self care
I expect it's my fault
somewhat
for assuming my kindness wouldn't be taken for granted
or assuming when being kind that some kind of kindness would be
    returned
assuming naively that he was good for me
when all along he was worse than the man across the hall
who he saw as some sort of a competition
when I saw the man across the hall as my best friend\

/he says I'm cute when I'm mad
aw... maybe that's why he pisses me off so much\

/they should ask you questions
they should want to listen to your stories
if they only talk of themselves
it's not a relationship\

/be cautious of your cup
be observant to who fills it
and notice who drinks from it too often
that you are left empty\

/why is it so hard for people to be good?
why aren't more people loyal?
everyone is incredibly selfish
and it's exhausting
everyone in this city is only looking out for themselves because no
    one is looking out for anyone else but themselves
and that is one reason this city is so chaotic
I know I am a cynic and I am a loner
but I know the value of a good friend
a value of being a decent human being
nobody wants to be fucking quiet for a minute
and look at the damn world around them
to let the world breathe for a second
to see the violence and sadness we're putting out
the ignorance we're putting out
the selfish hate we are putting out\

/*you care so much about other people,*
the musician said in a mocking tone,
because most people don't truly care about me
and I know how it feels to be alone in that aspect

/people who talk shit about their friends behind their back
are the people who want to neglect their own shit
cause they've been so deep in their shit they can't even smell it
    anymore\

/I've always felt as though my life has been lived constantly by two
    contradicting factors of myself,
a lone wolf
living amongst a violet fox
to the other woman who doesn't want any sort of relationship
to an openly hopeful girlfriend who wants to fall in love with her
    boyfriend who can't seem to love her or himself
alongside a girl with a boyfriend who still feels something much
    more passionate to a man who is not her boyfriend but has
    loved her more than any one in this city
lastly, to the dreaming girl, who wants her ideal career more than
    longing for any man

and yet I still struggle with knowing how to juggle these colliding
    characters
and which one of myself to let go of\

/I was across the hall at his place
sipping on some Hennessy
before the musician was supposed to come over
the man who I saw as yellow all that time ago
took me back to his bedroom,
I want to show you this,
he said as he searched in his desk drawer
he pulled out a red bent up notebook
and threw it on his bed next to me,
I want to make something…
I have ideas for maybe a little film or something
I wanted you to at least be in a few shots,
he remarked confidently
I looked through his notes
memorized by his ideas
when he laid a few photos of myself down on the inked page
I forgot you took these,
I said staring at the 35mm film photos
I held one photo up to the light,
oh, I forgot I named these after that story you told me,
he murmured timidly
I turned the picture over

and saw written in black sharpie
'the invisible ultraviolet',
I mumbled,
I've never told anyone else this...
that was two years ago
I can't believe you remembered that story,
he took a second
almost as if he were taken a back that I thought he would forget,
she meant a lot to you, I wouldn't forget what means a lot to you,
I stared at the black words
the invisible... ultraviolet,
I recited to see how it really sounded out loud,
how did you come up with that name for me?
I asked looking up at his caramel brown eyes,
it just seemed to fit, the way you described her and yourself with that
color... you hide yourself, but the ultraviolet, it's still there and
when people finally see that in you, they won't be able to take their
eyes off it,
he paused for a moment,
you're the invisible ultraviolet,
he said with his eyebrows raised and a big smirk to be more con-
vincing
within seconds he jolted his whole muscular body on top of me
swaying me back and forth engulfed in his arms
until I laughed a little,
will you help me make this video, please
I need your creative perspective,
he gave me a corny smile,
fine, if you make me a grilled cheese,

I told him flatly
that was already in the contract, kid

/I don't think the world is educated enough about mental health
and I don't hear much from the people who have dated someone
    struggling with mental health either
it's heartbreaking
it truly is heartbreaking
to watch someone you care about drowning in themselves
and how you want to fix them or save them
and I suppose
in some ways it can be selfishly difficult to grasp onto the fact of
    how badly you want to be their little light of happiness
to be their person that can let their sadness go
then when you can't and then when you realize this is bigger than
    you being what you think they need to be happy
and that happiness isn't one solid destination
happiness is a continuous process
happiness will always be a continuous process
you can start to feel as though you're not good enough
that you aren't good enough to make them happy
I can't imagine what is it like to be bipolar
I know I have mental health issues as well
but dating someone for 9 months with manic depression
no one seems to talk about how hard that is
to see someone you care for so much facing demons of themselves
I cannot begin to describe how defenseless you feel
to try so hard to save them
but a person's mind is so much more complex

and as I determine this topic
I remember laying in bed with him
after he seemed to have poured out his heart to mine
and it made me sink so low
to see him bleed in this way
and I told him,
all I want is to make you so happy,
and he looked at me with sunken in eyes
replying hollowly,
no one can save me

/I had a few people over to my apartment
I made my famous spaghetti and meatballs
drinks all around
of course the alcohol absorbed a little too much
the man across the hall and the musician got a little too drunk
finally had a conversation
at the end of it he exclaimed to my boyfriend,
she's amazing, one of the best people I know,
he looked over at me and smiled
while the musician kept his hesitant stare on my friend
and sneered,
is that why you never left your girlfriend for her?

/I argued with him to say,
he's my friend… nothing is going on between us,
and then he said to me,
I completely trust you…
I just don't trust him… that's why I don't want you guys hanging out
oh, how I've heard this line about a thousand times\
/*I trust you,*
the musician would say
I don't trust you yet,
I would tell him truthfully
there were things that I trusted about him
but I never trusted in him
I felt too strongly
that at some point
he'd emotionally kick the absolute shit outta me
and that thought terrified me most
because nobody has ever had that type of power over me
nobody
and that feeling was enough for me
to never trust in him\

/I realized quickly
that I love a musician
but dating a musician
is nothing I ever
ever

BLOOD ORANGE

I emphasize *ever*
would want to embark on again\
/I remember that night all too well
both of us were drunk again
slurring words that made no sense
but we laughed
sat on my bed
and he asked me if I would leave the musician for him

I recall that day often
if I had made the right decision
politely declining his yellow
for this deadhead musician\

/the beginning of summer
my girls moved in
I was extremely excited to live with my best friends
though that summer was not so sweet\

/it's so hard to fall for him
when some days he'd look at me
and I could feel that he felt nothing\

/sometimes I feel as though I am too loyal
in the wrong circumstances
I put him before myself
and I don't really know why
I sacrificed things for a person
whom I didn't really know enough\

/is this becoming love when I am the only one filling up your cup?
it takes two to make us
don't sleep on this cruise
there's a lot in these views\

/don't underestimate anybody
they'll never cease to surprise you\

/I remember when the man across the hall
was in the hospital
because a drunk driver hit him while he was walking in downtown
when I told the musician of this
I remember how he lightly laughed

and said,
karmas a bitch
we got into an argument when I mentioned I would visit him at
     the hospital
that passive aggressive attitude with the both of us lasted the whole
     day
and by that time I was so exhausted
and it hurt me that I decided not to visit him\

/you come to my table with nothing to eat
expecting me to spoon feed you love

/I asked the musician if we should break up
he started crying
I don't hate when men cry
in fact, I encourage it
just don't do it in my presence please\

/it usually takes a woman 8 times to successfully leave a relation-
     ship\

/the week I mentioned the break up
was probably the most love I got from him\

/I am so stubborn
I cannot give up
I am not a quitter\

/in an attempt to make our relationship stronger
or maybe to have a few good fake days of lovey moments
I invited the musician to be my date to my cousins wedding
this was two weeks after I'd recommended we break up
I must be crazy\

/at first
it sounded like a good idea
bring my boyfriend to my cousins destination wedding
that'll solve things
yah
no
don't do that
not when your family is Italian and crazy
not when the destination is got damn Arizona in the summer time

and your hot dress is drenched in boob and back sweat
and not when y'all were about to break up two weeks ago\

/now a days
I'm desensitized to backstabbing b*tches\

of these feelings that I do not speak upon-

/I heard those words
the same ones that kept me fearful of ever diving into another
    person
trusting them enough
to hold onto my belongings
to those words
how they sounded pouring out of his sour mouth
he left me with a sharp, distinct taste
brushed my teeth over a thousand times
the flavor of that day
still loiters there on my tongue
to these feelings...
I write about you...
which I rarely allow myself to speak upon...

this incident distorted my vision
with flashes of haunting hate
and painful sadness
then, no sounds were heard
silence took over this desert earth
for only my heart now echoing
pulsating with incredible pain
because I knew the day I was dreading for was here
as I heard the ground shake
woke me back to this day
I was done for now
the pack of wolves surrounded me
each one barked louder than the other
howling:
I told you not to trust him,
I told you not to feel anything,
I told you to leave him,
but you did not listen,
I wanted to argue back
to take off running in this seething, sultry desert sand
but I'd forgotten
that I was in my moms red high heels
and I had forgotten
it was my cousins wedding
and I could not act like this now
in the middle of this god damn dry, fucking desert
to be dumped by my boyfriend at my cousin's wedding
thirty minutes before the ceremony started
I had to pretend

I had to
but
in that moment
I wanted nothing else
than to allow myself to fill my heart with this incredible emptiness
I just wanted to let myself feel hurt
for once
it was a tremendous amount of effort to hide everything
than it was
to just let myself feel this shame

and in that moment
I was drained of my strength
my old trained power
evaporated in that dry heat
to shield myself from this hurt he had caused me
I did not want to be brave
at all
I did not want to be resilient
allow me to cry,
please,
is that too much?
to ask
to hurt?
to fill this desert
with my salted tears
release me from all of this
pain
and damage

embarrassment
hate
and rage
regret
and bitter loneliness
bring life
back to this dry place again
let me feel it
let me have this feeling
let it sink in
don't take this sadness from me
let me hold onto it,
don't let me continue to pretend,
I pleaded to myself
as I heard the wolves come charging back in
don't let him know that he hurt you,
they demanded
I turned my back to the wolves,
I want to feel this!
let me feel this,
I cannot be strong anymore,
I shouted to the pack
these tears were what could satisfy me
overflowing from my already overfilled glass

the wolves ceased their howling
while their yellow eyes stared silently back at mine,
she'd been alone for far too long,
she now needs our saving,

as they studied my hopeless, brown eyes
to their surprise
they were all starting to see more and more clearly
that for once,
I,
the lone wolf,
had no more fight left in me

steel emotions-

/I remember
when he broke up with me
I was surrounded by so many people
half of which I hadn't met till earlier that day
and the other half were people I knew my entire life
and yet I still had to pretend
I wanted to be alone
more than anything
away from the wedding
away from this desert
and allow myself to break
though my entire family kept telling me,
stop crying,
be happy for your cousin,
don't make this about him,
don't let him hurt you,

don't feel anything,
everyone except
for my dad
I saw him from across the room
and he could feel my misery
seeping through my mask
the one I would always wear
to appear courageous,
lets go,
he said firmly
reluctant for any sort of help
I decided to take his offer
for a while
we both said nothing
waiting out which one would melt first
then
my dad sheepishly asked,
so this was the first time you got your heart broken?
the assumed statement left me instantly offended,
he didn't break my heart,
I hissed back
oh...
so you've never had your heart broken before?
his familiar voice sounding foreign to my apprehensive ears,
no, no guy has ever broke me,
I pushed out a stubborn lie
one I still hold onto
sometimes
we went back to silence

we both kept our eyes on the scenery in front of us
I could not manage to look at my father in this moment
and he could tell that his daughter
wanted so badly to be brave
so he kept up the facade
for my sake
you know,
sometimes…
it's good to let yourself admit that you were hurt,
I stared stuck on those mountains
thinking to myself
of how I was raised by a father
whom was the king of suppressing his feelings
and next to him
on her throne
was my mother
the queen of stubborn emotions
I don't want to be weak,
I forced out of me
I've learned, Car,
sadness doesn't go away because you say you don't feel sad
at some point you need to let out your feelings
then they'll go away
eventually they'll go away… I promise,
he mumbled
and we still could not look at each other
two cynics
conversing about heartbreak
was not a smooth subject,

what happened when you had your heart broken?
I asked in somewhat of a taunting way
I expected him to respond with the same short-ended answer he
    had always given when I asked
as for my mother
she was an open book
it may have been a half fiction open book, but she still told a story
    nonetheless
as for my dad you couldn't find his book in any library on any old
    shelf anywhere
my father
he was crucially stubborn, a quiet soul
and my mom was the loudest spirit
you could not condense her into any closed jar
it took him a long paused moment
but then I watched as my dad unraveled
spitting out words as if I weren't on that car ride with him
I listened intently to his stories
ones which I used to beg him for as a child
but he would never dare speak on them
until then
hearing him pour out such vulnerable memories
which took up the whole car ride
still to this day
I've never seen my father so open
he had the bad habit of scrapping out his emotions
like black mold from a basement
I felt truly grateful
to have that moment with him

how he finally seemed to trust in me
even for a little while
and I thought to myself
how fascinating it is
to see
what can make
steel
break\

/as those paper cranes flew away
I was left there
standing alone\

5. ex girl friends

the red wedding–

/I sunk down deep in the desert sand
nothing for miles
except dirt and cactus and a stubborn sun
beating relentless on my heart
as I watched the dust kick away at the trail he left as he left me
    here
with nothing more than a glass of red wine from the wedding

a blank mind wondering why he wanted to end things
and left me to tell a whole gang of fury and fire as to why my boy-
    friend isn't here anymore
I craved the feeling to take off my heals
and run through this waste land
imagining myself stealing my cousin's horse
riding it down the road like the gypsy I am
and taking this bitch down with me as I crash
and I would ride off into the sunset
to California
and I would leave him stranded alone
on the top of some mountain range
strapped to a rock
with a one pistol shot
but my body could not move that swiftly
and those horses were surrounded by my family
tied into the wedding
and I could not begin to explain to them what just happened
until I saw my brother walking in the distance
we've been looking for you,
he announced,
what's wrong?
staring me down
and then he paused,
where is he?
my brother's voice began to trail off as he began to realize what was
    going on
he crotched down
met me eye to eye,

are you okay?
he asked in a slow softer way
I shook my head
feeling my eyes start to swell
as my heart tightened
and my lip began to quiver
but I held back just as much
to hide myself,
where the fuck is he? If he left you right before the wedding? I'm going
to fucking kill him!
my brother screamed,
fuck that bastard! he's a fucker, you don't want to be with anyone like
that, Carmen?
he said livid
that's when the numbness subsided
that's when all the tears came
that's when my cover was blown
that's when the humiliation to tell my whole entire family that my
boyfriend dumped me right as I am still processing that my
boyfriend dumped me before the wedding that I paid for his
broke ass to come to and then left me in this desert alone...
when he knew I already hated Arizona
but I guess
thank you, *musician*, for not dumping me in a place that I love
how gracious is your fucking timing\

/this breakup was honestly a bit harder than it was with my friend
    who had a girlfriend
only because he was my boyfriend
and everyone had heard about it
and I was with my Italian side at a wedding that he left me at
and those Italian's they drink a lot, eat a lot, and talk a lot
so sometimes silence is easier when you want to break down

When you've been dumped in a desert...
and it's your whole Italian family seeing you get dumped...
and don't try to cry in front of an Italian
because they don't do that shit
so I chose dark liquor and day time drinking to shut myself up
I decided to go to the pool with my cousins to dance my ass off
as I do so well
some ladies were staring at me
double fisting tequila shots in the hotel pool
after a few rounds of tequila
the waiter brought me a free shot
and I started crying to him, because I was so happy that were actual
    nice men in this world,
and unfortunately the nice man was in Arizona but what can you
    do?
want to hear a story? I said sniffing, as I brushed away the drunken
    free tequila shot tears
he laughed and said,
sure
I cleared my throat,
so I bought my boyfriend a plane ticket to my cousins wedding

and he dumped me and left me here alone
and I am miserable and I hate Arizona,
no offense,
so I need as much tequila as I can to dance off my sadness
because I am currently heartbroken
so don't think of me as an alcoholic weirdo
I'm just fucking heartbroken okay
and thank you for the free shot
and believe me
that was a big deal
since I was not even 21 at the time\

/I remember the first person I called while in Arizona
sitting on the heated concrete
outside of my cousins extravagant hotel
his yellow tone lit me up through the phone
his laughter and sweet temper calmed me
I knew he was the one to call\

/I mean…
to the people who said they were my friends
who claimed to have my back
then when I needed them

they sleep with my ex...
this generation is a bunch of backstabbing b*tches\

/I must've been an old soul
'cause loyalty is a gag to these kids\

/women will hurt you so much more than men
because women are calculated
they know exactly what they're doing
they've concocted the precise formula to beat your ass emotionally
and they mean it, they want it to fucking sting\

/I should have known
how apart of me could not let myself love him
because he was still focusing on how to love himself
so how could he love me?
if he can't even find love within himself\

/in your twenties you assume you know your friends
when you've really known them for a year
you don't truly know someone in one year
you'll get a taste of who they are
when put into a compromising position
trust me
wait till then\

/don't be shocked
if your friends switch up on you
this generation lacks selflessness\

/do not underestimate the power of an insightful woman
her intuition is something fewer men can manipulate\

/I was fortunate to have the friends that I did back then
because without them
I don't think I would have stayed in this city
I slept with Lala's cat for days in Hayden's bed with Hayden in bed
we would walk to the lake
drink pinot grigio on that technicolor tapestry
they could make me laugh when my throat was so dry from all this
    suppressed sadness I was so used to hiding\

/why is it so hard for me to let go
to leave a situation that no longer leaves me full
it's not the same anymore
I have to accept change
why is it so hard to accept that this is over
why is it so difficult for me to accept that people aren't as truly
    good as I thought them to be
why is it so difficult to let go of certain people
when it seems all too easy for them to let go of me\

/I told my friends while cruising that I had lost 10 pounds
Nany replied,
give me what you have, cause I could stand to lose some weight
I'm on this new diet,
I muttered,
it's called heartbreak, betrayal and food poisoning\

/I feel very deceived
to have found so many snakes
in what used to look like a beautiful garden\

/well, the thing about depression is
you get your sleep\

/I try to give people the benefit of the doubt
I push to feel their perspective
I empathize with their struggles
but if a person is neglecting to do a little bit of that for you
time and time again
move on\

/I don't know about you ladies,
but when I lose a friend
that's more heartbreaking than losing my man\

/and the thing about young snakes is
they shed their skin every two weeks...
often times it's hard to tell
which one they'll wear next\

/I'm not necessarily depressed…
I'm just not necessarily as happy as I should be\

/we're a sad generation
with happy instagram posts\

/and once again
the world and it's people
have left me utterly perplexed
on how to have any hope in any human being other than myself
dousing my heart with more and more cynicism\

/and then I got mad
when I replayed in my head over and over again
the words he chose to dump me with
he said,
I know you have trust issues
so I hope that you can find somebody else eventually
I hope I haven't ruined your thoughts about relationships for the rest of
    your life,

I realized getting out of that relationship
of how truly selfish he was
and that I am the kind of person who gives
that I need someone else who wants to give of themselves also
and then it made me laugh
how he had the audacity to assume that he had enough power
to shake me down to my core
and to assume that I was a weak enough woman
to never get back up from this, because *he* was the ultimate man to
    have shaken me down?
that goes to show
how he didn't care much to know who I truly am
I wouldn't ever give a man like that this kind of power
he certainly isn't half of a man to deserve to hold that power over
    me\

/women bleed way more than men
and yet
society has instilled in us
that we're the weaker sex\

/the first thing that really pissed me off was how my roommates
insulted my intelligence

fronting like they were as devious as Pablo Escobar
but I was always three steps ahead
they just didn't know it yet
to think they would assume I'd fall for their fabricated lies, or
    blocking me from certain posts would make me unaware of
    what was going on?
I don't even need to be Pablo or the DEA
to uncover the bullshit
because none of you are all too clever enough to know where to
    hide your shed skin
so maybe you're just the dead snake
under Pablo's boots\

/if you look at things and people
by the laws of nature
it makes more sense\

/I was alone
yet again
I never give myself enough time
to reflect on the healing process
what I wished I would've had
was someone to talk to
I want to go back to the past
to tell myself,

let this out, Carmen,
stop suppressing your feelings so much,
but when I moved in with the people who I thought were my
    friends in this city
they decided to become closer to my ex
hanging out with him on a regular bases
when it was only two months after he had hurt me
it was hard living with friends who I felt betrayed me
laying down with whom I saw as my enemy
leaving me once again
to bleed out the darkest shades of violet
that no one else saw
besides myself\

/if your friend
or roommate
gets dumped
please don't hang out with their ex
it should go without saying
but I guess in some cases
it fucking goes with saying
don't hang out with my ex\

/it's difficult to heal when your roommates are
legitimately devaluing information about you
to your ex boyfriend
and even though this city is the third biggest
you can still manage to hear what the assholes have to say about
    you\

/I am so exhausted from having to hide my emotions from my
    friends
I'm exhausted from rescuing myself alone
I just want to have a moment
where somebody else pulls me aside from my mind,
and tells me,
put down your sword,
you don't need to protect yourself so much,
because I am with you now
and you'll be safe here

/back then I was so composed
so careful of how I looked
or how I was perceived by people who were hurting me
at the time
I had to show no emotion towards them
I could not give into letting them know I was drowning in heart-
    break
I couldn't let my roommates see me crumble

because they would go and tell him
and the things I had heard him saying about me
we're so insulting that it made me feel even more sick to my stom-
    ach
I would never want to call for help\

/my pride
and my ego
were too big for my head\

/how can I heal
when my home is infested
with fucking snakes\

/I am a loner at heart
I don't care to get close to much of most people
and yet,
I believe my biggest fear
is ending up completely alone\

/I said no
so many times
that the word
had diminished from my mouth
and instead
it continued to come out tangled and muffled
I used all of my strength to keep him off of me
slashing at him
relentlessly
like these high hides
but that did not phase him
using his slurred drunken words to manipulate this situation
and he lasted as long as 3 minutes
but these three minutes hit me still
while my cries were completely numb to his selective hearing
the pain
he was inflicting upon me
would stay
rooted deeply
left these marks on my stolen body
that was something
he would never understand
something I will never be able to gain back
how it felt
to be taken down
like a wild animal
left for the dead
for another person to pick at my flesh
and as he shut the door behind me

left alone to cry on my own
for what he decided to use me for
men will never understand
unless this happened to them
how it feels to have someone force themselves onto you
defenseless and used
that feeling of loss
is engrained in us
for eternity
especially marked in our minds of battered men
and as he forced me to become silent
he took me down
right along with him\

/why weren't you here?
I needed you,
and you weren't here,
I screamed to her
feeling my stomach tighten,
I have nobody in this city
nobody
I needed you,
I said as my voice began to weaken,
I would go back to Minnesota…
but you aren't there anymore either,
I whispered to myself\

/I wish more straight males
would know the feeling
the wound that festered and lasts on someone who is a victim of
      sexual assault\

/I am still processing the emotional trauma
of my body being taken
but this would not be the last time
I would feel this\

/I was dealing with losing my roommates friendships
because of a narcissistic guitarist
and trauma from a sexual assault
it always seems to start with smoke everywhere
to one giant fire
suffocating
so many nights went without much sleep
isolating myself from the world
Archer and wine became my best friends
while my roommates became my strangers whom I shared an
      apartment with
I kept myself composed
nobody knew I was suffocating\

/trauma does not sleep
only the human tires out\

/I distracted myself
going out on a very far limb and applying for a job I had no back-
    ground in
at the last place I expected to end up
below deck
on the biggest yacht
docked at one of the most monumental tourist attractions in Chi-
    cago
working along side characters
That Quintain Taratino
would love to write about\

/working in a kitchen
is psychotic
and I love it
the moment I stepped onto that gigantic ship
and down to the kitchen
I saw so many people of color
so many walks of life
so many characters

I was immediately intrigued
I heard people on the line cussing back and forth
my boss wore a gold chain over his chef coat
everyone was either laughing or fighting
the cooks would joke and play off of our personalities
finding creative ways to make work fun
they would scream across the kitchen
walk off the line when they wanted to
spark up a cigarette if they needed to take the edge off
I mean…
I could not believe it
all the while
they were still cooking
hands would fly every which way
trays in the oven every other five minutes,
plating as fast as their hands could text
all the while talking shit
it was like a comedy show
with chefs
I've never in my life witnessed interactions to this degree besides
    on TV
I never thought I'd be working in an environment like this
and as a writer
my mind was booming with ideas\

South Side-

/my coworker asked me once,

do you believe in God, Carmen?
and I asked him,
do you believe in God?
and he said to me,
there's no God here
if you'd seen what I've seen
you'd know…
God gave up on us
a long time ago

/I filled my stomach with work
every day till my legs ached
until my toes didn't want to bend any longer
so that all I could think about was going home to smoke and sleep
and I would walk all the way from the pier to my apartment
I focused on never being home
spending the night at friend's places
anywhere besides my own bed
avoiding my apartment
yet again
it's really one of the worst feelings
as a young adult
to be paying for such an expensive apartment
and yet…
feeling incredibly uncomfortable in your own home\

/I was so exhausted from being sad
the emotional toll was too hard to bare
I was especially tired of being so depressed over people who did not
    care to see me happy\

/I wasn't expecting anyone else to put me back together besides
    myself\

/but karma will bite them in the ass
harder than my words will
so I'll just sip on my coffee
bite my tongue on this one
go on with my life
because they'll create their own storm from their own wrong agen-
    das to serve only themselves
and meanwhile I'll keep striving to do better
and chose greater friends\

/I kept myself composed
for months
I used to hear my roommates talk about how lazy I was
that I slept too much
that I acted angry or rude to them
they were lucky I was half Arab

if I were full blooded Italian
it'd be a different story\

/there is magic
in those who love you so much that they see beauty in the parts of
    you that you see as
broken\
/she told me,
go ahead, Carmen, cry to the moon
see if the sun can answer to your sadness

/I cannot think anymore
my mind is ruptured
dreams I've wanted to achieve
spilling out of me
like loose leaf tea
to the floor
wanting more
but never satisfied with the score
short lived
once at war
bones breaking in
teeth clenched
b*tch, want to take this hit
my mind is the thing I battle most with
sword to my chest

breathing in and out
panic attack
feels like a heart attack
the sword never cuts too deep
but it does leave a few marks on me
to be reminded of how badly I want this
of how much it is killing me to want this
yet it has the power to keep me living\

/most adults I've come to know seem to tell me,
being a kid is hard being an adult is harder,
in my own experience I've learned that this is so far a very true
        statement
but it's difficult in many different forms for any child
for a child's life to not be difficult
for many different reasons
but it's especially difficult when you're quote on quote *different*
because as children we are taught to look in patterns
that there is always one right answer to solve this
to make sense of things
for it to fit
and if doesn't go in the pattern
or if it looks unfamiliar it's usually wrong
when you look different as a child
or come from a different background
or your brain thinks differently than most
those different kids have it the hardest
in my opinion

I remember feeling so different that it excluded me from the nor-
    malcy of this quote on quote *childhood life*
though
now that I've grown up
my childhood, it still affects my adulthood
in many ways
as I am sure it does for anyone
though most people will separate it and say they were just children
    and now they're grown
but I say it's all relative
your childhood is what shaped you
it is not gone now simply because you've aged
it is apart of you
I look at the reasons of how I saw myself as different
how others deemed me as different
and I've answered with,
so… what can I make from all of this?\

/I worked three jobs
hustling
that's how you get over a situation
shake your ass
and make some money\

time to be selfish–

/surrounded by these never ending skyscrapers
sounded by these never ending noises of urgency that I've seemed
   to numb out
I longed to be way up in the mountains
where those forgotten wild flowers grow
and I could sit still for a little while
a tab on my tongue
to rediscover who I am
not to be distracted by every step I take
and hear nothing of these sounds from this chaotic city
senseless to this petty drama
and life
I want to live full again
take me from this city for a moment
and give me the mountains
and the sea
I need to see something beautiful again
I need to see myself as beautiful again\

6. a girl goes to Paris

/so I chose to hide myself from everyone in this city
all of them
until a group of friends I had since my first month in Chicago and
    my neighbor
they came to my apartment unannounced
grabbed my hand and pulled me out of the place where I was
    hiding
and they took my sword from my apprehensive closed fist

and they waited until I was comfortable to take my mask off
as they handed me a blunt and a glass of wine
and let my voice be the only thing heard
they listened to what I chose to hide from everyone
because I was so humiliated and so sad and so alone
and then they emphasized to me,
we're all here for you,
no one will hurt you anymore,
that was all I wanted for so long
but I was afraid of being too vulnerable
and since that day
those two girls that were my friends
and that one man who attempted to break me
they could never come close to hurting me again
I didn't let them
and it showed me
that while there are a lot of fake friends out there
that's when you see the real boss ass b*tches shine\

/the world never took much of a knee
to my mountains
that I climbed
which many rarely knew of
the world continued on it's way
and I was moving so fast
Batman couldn't catch me

I numbed all of my possible pain
stuffed it into my cup
and drank it down
remembering some in the morning
marching forward still\
/the girl with the violet eyes called me one day,
she told me of this place
of far away lands
of languages I adored to speak
I longed to be there\

/April came calm
the crisp air lightened my dark hair
the sun illuminated my fickle face
turned my cheeks to a pale pink
with flustered eyes of deep, dark brown
I saw an opportunity
of which I couldn't pass
booked a flight to Paris
left my jobs on hold for that moment
to ran away to France\

/Paris,
I have appreciation for these cobblestoned streets
fresh baked bread through the market place
coffee in my hand
a glass of pinot an hour later in the park
take a stroll down the river walk with me
teach me how to fall in love\

/you wanted less of a woman
I will never be less for a man
I will be all of myself and then some\

/traveling through the streets of Paris
with my best friend on my arm
a cigarette
passed between the two of us
as we stared up at the black sky
at the illuminating Eiffel Tower
blinking of diamonds and dancing stars
we shared a night in his flat just a few blocks away
drunk on summer wine
and laughter
she fell in love in Paris
I saw my best friend in her old fashion glamour

BLOOD ORANGE

her violet eyes kissed Europe goodnight\

/I can rule this kingdom just fine on my own\

/beautiful old buildings
they whispered of stories untold
climbed inside my mind
just to tell me more
the streets of Paris seemed to dance
like dazzling lightening bugs
no streets were abandoned
women strutting down the cobblestoned streets in their Gucci
    Couture
a meal isn't served without a glass of wine
men generous and refined
round windows
steel balconies
beautiful people
beauty in Paris is all that I see\
/I could walk for days in Paris
and I would never need my headphones again
since the street brings me my music
there was so much to see

this other world consumed me
bringing out the brightest shades of violet\

/the food was incomparable
the wine was lemony and crisp
puffy, white and whimsical clouds
sauntering across the milky blue sky
the river was consumed with people
merchants selling their finest handmade crafts
buildings of crown mold and gold
dripping down it's ancient spin
I longed to stay here for the rest of my life\

/clubbing in Paris
is no comparison to the nightlife in Chicago\

/I was not concerned about finding a man
I was concerned about living\

/the girl with the violet eyes
had butterflies in her stomach
for the man in Paris
I could tell they both adored each other
I was happy for her\

/after a few weeks in Paris
we took a train to Angouleme, France
the girl with the violet eyes knew of a gay designer couple
whom lived in a 15th century castle
they fed our belly's Italian wine and spaghetti
fresh baked bread from the town of Angouleme
riding our bikes around the small city
known for it's comic character influence
wild flowers and classic cars rolled up and down the hills
the language beautiful and addicting
the smell sweet and somber\

/a year ago,
I was in Arizona
crying over a man
I didn't even really want to indulge in
now I am in the south of France

living in the top of a 15th century castle
over looking the wild horses and extensive fields
of wild, red poppies
with my best friend from Minnesota

/I found myself flirting with France
adoring her old architecture
and French graffiti
each told a story about her
as you walked through the streets

/you haven't really seen a person
until you travel with them\

/as we evolve on this planet
we need to make sure Mother Earth is okay too\

/homes painted in technicolor
dreams

whimsical wind chimes hung loosely around the windows
cherries and blue berries sold fresh around the corner
no man was on my mind
I was capsulated by this exquisite country side
by the language
from the food
to the wine
and the poppy fields that roamed
to the street animals that gnawed at my heels
I was captured by life here
nothing else from my past mattered
I didn't have room in my suitcase for that extra baggage\

/I've fallen in love,
she said
as she sat in the windowsill
in that old castle
with who?
Paris\

7. a girl comes home

/it's been a long enough time
long enough for me to thank the universe
thank you to myself
and to the places I went that allowed me to reform,
to the coffee that kept me well motivated
and to the people who helped me get over the ones who I needed
    to let go of, to let go of the wounded emotions
to better my life

thank you for showing me that I had the strength to get over these
    challenging times
so that this is no longer sadness
now that I've let go
I can start something new\

/thank you,
to my friends and family
the one's whom bathed me in rainbows,
when I felt as though I had no more color left in me
it was such a relieving reminder
of what it felt like
to swim in full color\

/I knew she was a keeper
the first time I met her
she helped me move out of my cursed apartment\

BLOOD ORANGE

the American dream–

/life does not halt for anyone
after nearly two months in my excursion to France
I needed to return to my old American life
I had to move out of my South Loop apartment
and to the west side of Chicago
living amongst my exquisite drag queen best friend
and my favorite blonde singer\

/I was glad
that I was a girl
who needed the city to breathe\

/there is no other friend
like the bartender
at 2pm
at my local bar down the street from my house
who smiles and talks to me
while he hands me a beer
I leave my crescent moon lipstick on the can\

/you'd only find friends like these in Chicago
I am so blessed to have a family here
they're my safe space
they're my night life
they're my sisters
my brothers
my trusted soldiers
I love them so much
my world would not be the same without them in it
I thank this chaotic city
for bringing me the most genuine people

/if it's in my body, than it's in my hands to decide\
/the violence in this city does not sleep a wink
but it gives Chicago a harsh name
for all it's beauty that these Chicagoan's make
she does not get enough credit for her artwork
or for her glamour\

/I should've never been afraid to ask my friends for help
I didn't want to be a burden

but you should never feel like that when it comes to your true
    friends
true friends want to help you heal\

/I've learned all too well
about beautiful pieces of art breaking
to create something more extraordinary\

/time
friends
projects
working
traveling
cooking
these are healing techniques\

/I see tangerine trees
growing in and out of my beautiful mind\

/I have to
remind myself that
some people do not rationalize or think
the same way as I do\

/uplift your friends for what makes them different
we are characters
no story is good without a diverse cast\

/you can get through months of war
if you have true friends who will stand with you\

/we all need to learn how to be more empathetic and patient with
    one and other\

/we are different
that is what makes us beautiful

stop trying to change other people
stop trying to limit other people
stop trying to fit other people into your mold
let them live the life they want to
do not judge others for certain lifestyles
you will never know the choices they had\

/all are welcome here
as long as you're striving to be your authentic self
I cannot ask for anything more of you\

/we wound the ones closest to us when we are insecure
because we know it'll evoke emotion from them
we selfishly like to be reminder that we are important\

/y'all need to learn how to stop being so passive aggressive
be a little more confrontational with your feelings\

/young people spend so much time on their phones
that they can't decipher real human emotions\

/men call it an attitude
when a woman puts a man in his place\

/other than a woman's body
food is art that you can taste\

/remember, ladies,
fake ass women *cannot* break a bad ass b*tch like you
they don't have the strength to
it's not in the cards for these fake women…
just like *the house*
the house always wins, baby
the house
always
fucking wins\

/do not give up on who you are
and especially do not let your head convince you that these tempo-
    rary feelings are permanent
because this sadness will subside
and if you put good out to the world
the world will give you its goodness back tenfold\

/there are two types of people
the ones thankful for what they do have
and the ones starving for what they don't have\

/I think that it is good if you have doubts
it should mean that you're recognizing your own self worth
because you deserve someone who would eventually offer you the
    sun
not someone who'd give you a handful of sand
arguing that he had just given you the stars\

/I manifested a trip to California
with my girl in the left seat rider

she calls me a spit fire
coming up just to get you lost in your mind
right beside ya
had my dreams inspired
by California\
/sativa stained lipstick
seemed to have slapped me in the face before I could take a hit of it
satin leather seated kisses
put me in your ride
California on my mind
Tyler The Creature on the high speed player
took me to clouds of paradise
then doubled back again for a second ride
palm trees sway away as I stray away from these bad vibes
high stakes for high standards
where'd you find those manors
left them out with your old PBR cans and hammered friends
I have California on my mind
so don't waste my high
aviator looking glass
fill mine to the brim
I'll take more than I asked
I've got much to say
much more to relay
California palm tree bedsheets on my mind\

/I spent the week in California
seeing musicians I've longed to hear in person
along side two new guy friends
and my Chicago home girl\

 /I met him amongst the mourning sun
November hit
and I was born again

blooming
he was different
than the ones before
quiet and subtle
gentle
he was light blue
curly dark hair
almond brown eyes
freckles dusted his checks
aviator sunglasses to match the heat
though he was far away from where I sleep\

/my heart knew before my realistic head could justify this attraction
I trusted him
because he was my best friends best friend
she would vouch for him
that was what I needed in those times
someone to back him up
otherwise my trust issues would have been too much
however,
my intuition told me he was someone to trust in\

/California had been burned in my mind
my time spent there was incredible
I could have traveled for weeks with these people
sort time I became entangled in him
and here\

dyslexia-

/I was told
multiple times
from multiple people
as a young, dreaming girl
that I could never be a writer
because of a road blocking learning disability

never tell a child
that she is not a storyteller
to those whom showed me doubt at a young age
I will write to you now
of how I am a storyteller
still to this day I am what you said I could not be
I am a writer
this is who I am
who I have always been
do not presume to take my identity away\

/I had routine in my life
stabilization for once
my friends were beautiful and glowing
I was getting my groove back in writing
working till 2 in the morning
on the yacht
faceTiming the California man while I walked to the bus stop
wasn't a bad life\

/leaving school was a difficult decision
there is such a negative stigma on a college drop out
my extended family read me to filth
they weren't copasetic to my plan
realizing I'd rather get paid to learn than pay to learn
I was being taught life skills at my jobs
even though that wasn't exactly the career path I chose to take
I wanted to be a writer
I wanted that more than anything since I was young enough to
    dream
but school didn't teach me much other than procrastination and
    winging it
however, if it were classes I was interested in than of course that
    was a different story
but to have a good class you need a well advised teacher
many of them weren't well advised surprisingly for college
and in america

we put such a high price tag on fucking education and the older
    generation really wonders why my generation is getting stupid-
    er and stupider?
they wonder why the incarceration rates are so high?
I don't need to walk the path of an American life
the way america claims their way to success
drowning in student debt
coming out with a piece of paper I'll most likely barely use besides
    to flaunt on my resume
I have gained all of my knowledge
from life experiences
from my own hard work and creativity
I've gotten my food photography in online articles, and paper mag-
    azines from working my ass off at my photography jobs
from being a social butterfly and making those connections
from listening to others
from applying, applying, and applying
working and working
I've learned more in the kitchen than I did back in high school
the city teaches you whether you want to listen or not
you can learn from your experiences more than you will at school
but that's just my opinion\

/I'll be working my entire life
on segueing the stigma of mental health to something more posi-
    tive

we wonder why we're all messed up
when the world wants us to swallow our sorrows
stuff our emotions down our throats
or choke on all the debt of medical bills
it's not necessarily your civic duty to be a therapist to your friends
      or family
however, talk to them
be that person to listen when they need it
mental health is extremely important
many times we neglect to see the signs in other people who're
      struggling
try your best to be diligent
also be there for yourself
nearly everyone struggles with mental health
give yourself that time that you need
be gentle with yourself when you know you need to be\

/I need to work on being kinder to myself
I can be a nasty bitch sometimes
and yet
I would never say these things to my friends
so why am I saying this to myself?\

/we get critical about ourselves in the wrong problems we have\

/he was the first man that I thought was better than seeing yellow\

/I was still friends with the old neighbor
he was still yellow as can be
but I saw him in a different light
and I rarely saw him anyhow
he had been single for 10 months now
he was better this way\

/it was like taking a xanax when I was with him
I was so comfortable
and so happy and chill
I had no worries
no anxiety when I was with him
I missed my California man\

/it is beautiful when you can comfortably
share your feelings with someone\

/what a gorgeous place to be
when I don't have to worry
or put strain on myself because of another person
when we're both comfortable together\

/strive to be with a person
whom lifts you up
who fills your cup with Fiji water
someone who shares their wealth
as do you
someone who hustles
and motivates you
to be the best version of yourself\

/he motivated me to be better
uplifted me in my art

he showed me compassion from so far away
he made me feel beautiful without having to tell me\

/I believe we know what is right and what is wrong
I believe we know in our hearts
when we are in the right place\

/I don't believe the media
talks about the suffocating effects of misogyny in the kitchen
I've had male cooks tell me,
I won't take orders from a woman,
now, one of the men who said this
had a tattoo on his arm that said,
fuck you
so
if that doesn't say much I don't know what does
besides the kitchen hires the craziest f-ing people\

/I can now accept to sink into this room-temperature water
I have been longing for this bath
the light reflects onto my naked skin
I feel the love of these gentle waves
come to console me
to consume me
wrap me up in their tide
to cleanse me from my past body
take away these tired tears I spared in those heavy nights
release me from old heartache
and my future that I fear
so that I may sink
finally

in my heart
and in my swallowed soul
to my anxious spirit
to my beautiful body
I can sink
finally
into him
and into my passions
I feel comfortable
in letting go of myself now
this is a new transition
strange to the touch
on my uneasy
fragile figure
but for once
I don't hold that familiar feeling
of being incredibly scared in what was once
a very tense and agitated body
and as I take my golden armor off for myself
and for him
now
he can know
what it feels
to touch raw skin\

/back of house
is the best in house\

/food is one of my soulmates
cooking is one form of my self therapy
falling in love with the flavors
serenading with the smells
how my rhythm with my Kuro reflects my artwork
I take the time to make my meal
as if I were cooking for my last supper
simmering in the moment as I create my art\

/as I've grown up
I've come to realize
how often I see my mother in myself
in many times I didn't think imaginable\

/we're all just bullshitters to our own devices\

/why do we seem to project immense amount of energy on the
    people who've hurt us?
why are we so obsessed with being accepted
that we neglect the people who've never asked of us to prove our
    self worth
we focus so god damn much on the ones who've walked away
rather than the ones who have always been there\

/I remember watching them
all most everyone in that kitchen wanted the title
chef
they all envied Frank
for his gold rings
and shinny things
they wanted that apartment in the sky
the one in Streeterville
my coworkers hustled they worked so hard
dedicated
and they all wanted to be somebody
somebody in the kitchen
and I wanted to be somebody else
I wanted to be a writer
but I was stuck in that kitchen\

/as I get older I understand her more
why she's frustrated
why I felt the need to earn approval from people more confident
I know why she defends herself
though it taught me to hide my feelings
but to listen and to comprehend human emotion
I can admit that I've developed some abandonment issues
when she left
always afraid she would never come back
though, she would never admit the fears she had
I adored her glamour stories
of the old days in LA
when she was invited to Madonna's party
or when she worked with Yoko Ono
she's been my first and longest supporter
and as I get older
it makes me sad to think
that I'll never fully understand my mom
though, I want her to fully understand me\

/I don't know what it is
but he has me
somewhat
wouldn't allow another man to hold me up
but he's got me down
not no "down b*tch"

but I suppose I'll stick around
string wrapped around my bony finger
to remind him that I'm still there
I let him stay close somewhat
when it's warm here
when this city stays awfully cold here
I do not see old reflections of myself
I do not see the face of the other men who've tried to rip me apart
he is clean from my soul
washed me out in these heating coals
I can replenish myself here\

/the world spun and shook
I truly believe
it through us together
feel like 1969
California weather
I feel you there
and I know
nobody can take this from me
feeling as though the sun radiates on my olive skin
your words spread over me
like maple syrup or honey
smooth and glossy
he brings water to this dry desert
flowers to my wicker park window

he brings light to my erupting spirit
food to my starving soul
he brings me the ocean
when I've only seen snow\

/I remembered a few things I learned from my blunt uncle
he said,
tequila first, because don't deal with your problems sober,
and,
there's always gonna be an asshole where ever you go, in any relation-
    ship, in any job, in some friends, so figure out which one is the
    asshole and use it to your advantage
and if you can't find any
than I guess that means you're the asshole,
most of his advice occurred during our Sunday dinners
back in Minnesota
Uncle Louie lived with us for awhile
Grandma and Grandpa lived up the block
and they'd come over with their homemade pizzelles
and I remember how Louie got dumped by his girlfriend of three
    years, which was a long relationship for him
he was heart broken
though, the tequila never told him that
and she wanted nothing to do with him
and then one Sunday Dinner
he got several calls from his ex

and suddenly we could see on his face how the entire game had just
    changed
and he used that to his advantage
every time she'd call he'd hang up and smirk as he took a sip
my soft spoken grandma murmured,
Louis, why don't you answer her? She's called you so many times. Aren't
    you worried?
he said matter of factly,
if I don't answer she'll think I don't care,
grandma looked at him stubbornly,
exactly, so answer the phone,
his raspy voice continued on,
that's exactly why I'm not answering the phone, ma,
then he looked across the table at my brother and I
the sound of Louie's obnoxious ring tone took the tone of that
    Sunday dinner
he continued to eat, feeling more content each time his phone rang
well, if you're not going to answer turn it off at least,
my mom said to her brother,
he flashed us his burner phone until the screen went blank,
hopefully it's not something important,
my grandma said muffled as she poked at her farfalle
Louie cleared his throat,
listen,
he directed his one gimpy eye towards my brother and I,
the best way to defeat your enemies
is creating the illusion that you don't give a fuck about revenge,
his gestures reminded me of Spongebob when Spongebob made a
    rainbow out of his hands with 'imagination,'

or more importantly, you don't give a single flying fuck about them all
   the way around
because if they see you sweat
if they think you care
they'll assume they've won
so once you perfect the illusion that they don't mean shit to you
without even recognizing it eventually they won't mean shit to you
and then, without them even realizing
they'll start to go crazy,
wondering why the fuck they don't have that hold on you like they used
   to,

he pointed his finger at us,

then you'll see them sweat
and let them sweat a little
'cause they fucked you over
The thing about humans… They're so consumed with being wanted
once you don't want them
they want you even more,

he dangled his burner phone at the whole table,

the only thing is… you cannot ever let them see that you care
and eventually you won't need to pretend to not care, because you'll see
   that they don't matter anymore
They lost you
You dodged the bullet
They took the bullet
You didn't even pull the trigger
You just loaded the gun and they did this all to themselves
So let her fucking sweat…
because she'll need a whole fucking ice bath after I'm through with her

/there is no good verses evil in this world when it comes to humans
everybody has good and evil in them
there isn't one person on this earth whom hasn't done something
      sinful
don't go around throwing stones at glass houses when yours is built
      of the same material\

/listen to your grandparents
listen to their stories
because they can tell you things with full heart
something the internet can't do to their extent\

/a person out there could tell you that they watched their father die
they could paint you the picture
or even not
just simply telling you is enough to understand how tragic of a
      situation that is
there are no words
but nobody would ever ever understand the feeling your body got
      when you watched your father die
nobody would understand the trauma the heartache
no one could understand the loss
unless they've had that happen

so why when we hear about a woman being raped
do we not get the same emotional respect as if we were to hear of
    someone dying?
many women have been raped
manipulated
abused
sexually assaulted
so I found it extremely aggravating
when a man tries to belittle a woman who's gone through this sort
    of trauma
when you hear someone has experienced this
people should understand that this is a traumatic event
that this is not okay
but a man will never ever understand it until they have gone
    through this
they would not understand how her body feels
how her mind has been altered from this tragedy
rape and abuse is real
being slut shamed is real
no man understands this clearly because it seems to be so common
yet pushed under the rug
nobody will understand the severity of it till it has happened to
    their body till they have been taken advantage of
it makes me sick when I see men defending other men who have
    done this crime to women
its continuing the cycle
that needs to end\

/back in college
I came across serial rapists
and the school did nothing about this
that's the sad, twisted truth
is if women come out publicly about their traumas it is consistently
     met with utter contempt
and verbal violence against the woman
this needs to change\

/I had a boy from my college come to one of my apartment parties
when he was not invited
he sat at my dinner table with his hands together
palms extended
a smirk on his face
as he told me,
sit down, Carmen,
we have something to talk about
I had called out his friend for raping my other friend from college
this happened two years ago
and he came over to relay a message
of how I lied on his friend being a rapist
and that I was lying about it so that he couldn't get with any of my
     friends?
this immature child
legitimately
came to my house uninvited

to tell me that my friend who was raped by his roommate and
    comrade was lying about it
he told me of how she wanted it
that she and I made the story up so that they would look bad
and that I am still telling the story to my friends so that he can't
    get with any girls?
yes, you're hearing this correct
he had the fucking gumption
to come and sit at my table
where I eat
to spit out this disgusting talk
to make a mockery of her trauma
I told him,
stand up and get the fuck out
how dare you tell me I'm lying about that
and either way
I never told my friend about the rape
she never wanted you in the first place, regardless of your friend who's a
    rapist
that's all for now, folks-

/I hope if I ever become a mother that I have a boy
so I can at least have one man in this world who I can whoop his
    ass into real shape to treat women with some god damned
    respect\

/I have been the victim and I have been the manipulator
I have left people I care about and I have been left by people who cared
    for me
I have made mistakes and hurt people unintentionally and the people
    who I've cared about have made mistakes unintentionally that have
    hurt me
I have been the accused and I have been the accuser
I have used people and I have been used by people\

/is it really that hard to become a decent human being?
or to at least work on evolving into a better human being
should not be so difficult\

if I did something, say it to my face-

/y'all are worse than a god damn sewing circle
why don't you guys come together, piece up what little informa-
    tion you've found about this story, think about it for a second,
    conjure up some interesting twists, then call me and I'll see if
    you got it right\

/but a lot of people my age
need to learn how to toughen the hell up
me included\

/my father said to me once,
what drives us is either love or fear
which car are you in?\

when it comes to being a b*tch–

/she said there was little in difference between her and I when it
    came to being a b*tch
and I said to her,
no... the difference between you and I, is that you are a snake, and I am
    the lion\

/*life is a game...* she said, sitting there lazy on that bar stool,
and we're either pawns or queens in it
As she handed me that chess piece\

/in my mind
a little bit too much\

/I woke one day in paradise
surrounded by violet skies
salt water nails
touched through my Lebanese curls
tan skinned glowed
floor to ceiling windows
show me what I don't know
I half achieved what I've been working my whole life for
the thing that those type A adults told me I could not fully grasp
    in my small little hands
I cannot describe this feeling
it's like coming home
after working 12 hours in downtown, Chicago
sitting next to my best friend on the couch
joint between our fingers
narcos on the projector
I am
living,
da'ling\

8. messy girls

/I checked in with hell and heaven
they said I still had some time left to kill\

/I was quite confused
her face said,
I'm gonna throw up
but her ass said,
let's fucking party

when lusting or doing drugs-

/but these feelings
of euphoria
or of empty sadness
both of these
are temporary feelings\

/she let herself go
falling effortlessly
through these shattered pieces
of what was once her body
through sharp glasses
a plastered out face
she dipped her little pinkie finger
in the white girl powder
saw in her eyes
sadness that had been submerged

now it's above her
looked in the mirror
getting louder
bolder
a lion in the crowd became of her\
/she lived for the moment
sometimes too much\

/she washed her sins down
with a glass of tequila
every night
white towel wrapped around her wet hair
with coffee on the counter
and a cigarette in her fingers
she stands out on her small balcony
had a party there last week
over looks the city
she rarely sleeps
speaks easily to men who lust over her
she can't seem to get a break
stacks of benjamin's in her pillow case
glossed over eyes hidden behind her blacked out shades
with one nail gone
she bites down on it
so you cannot see her flaws\

/figuring him out
letting him expand
watching us absorb each other
from my thoughts to his
from his stories
learning what makes him unconventionally happy
how he orders jimmy johns when he's hung over
or when he was 10 what sales tactics did he use while working his
    lemonade stand
to his prom date who was secretly a lesbian\

/think with your eyes wide open
you see more than what you choose to hear\

/I found myself getting lost so easily
being caught up in trying to find every moment
thrilling\

/I was always myself
I might have pretended around certain people

but do not be mistaken
I've always known
who I am
deep down
somewhere\

pretty little lady lies-

/I am
a ballerina
in disguise
I've come to play it well,
for these men who come to see me
rarely seem to notice
how I lie
that I play a role
how I pretend
that I hide
muffled in these sheets
as I play the ballerina
in his dreams
how can they not see
after awhile,
that these are sounds of pain
not of pleasure

I watch as he just sits there
so I take control
I dance my heart out
rhythm and soul
roping him in with my curly black hair
red nails tripping down his body like a woman with red bot-
      toms on
and long legs walking down North and Broadway
eyes he can't stop gazing at
and my voice
it marinates
his 20 minute meal
with pizzazz and kick
he won't forget
how I taste
I know how these men work
now that I am up on this stage
this spot light blinds me
I shield my eyes from this pain
I've caused myself to feel this shame
now it's too late to leave
thought this is what I wanted
I think this every time
but it is not what I need
and yet, I know this
every time
even so, I give him my best performance
and false show of exuberant happiness
at the end of it

as I take my bow
and collect my profits
but he does not seem to notice
that I feel nothing good from all of this
he doesn't think much of my feelings
in relation to this incident
because I suppose
I should be incredibly simple to please
and there for,
this is what becomes expected
to men
from a woman
in bed\
/do not forget
how I was there for you
when you had no one
now that you have someone
I am no one to you\

/champagne and cocaine
order go-puff
lil' lo mien
he says she gives good brain
mama's mad
'cause it's her birthday
I unintentionally got shit faced

no excuses were made
just a tool bag
in the tool shed
leave me out
garden go to bed
fucking sleepy head
running through life
like cocaine lines
get your mind right
shame on the turn pike
Lil Bit said,
it's a street fight
Lo Lane left that night
garden hoes water these hoes
run some errands
go to Lowes
took a few blows
did some blow
that's how life goes
when you running these bros\

/I said,
I'm not a hoe

/I look sexy for me
not to get cat called
I'am not your hound dog\

/and as I seem to do so well
there I sail
off into a oblivion
traded my free night for a fifth
handle of Jack Daniel's
need a spliff
but can't stand the smell of tobacco anymore
so I let the mary sit
and he tries to sit in my mind
yeah, he can manage to fit
eventually I spiral off again
off into oblivion
give me a bottle
some of that white girl powder
so I can make it happy that much longer
which seems to settle me for the time that I am bothered
can't catch a break
so I catch a thrill
hopefully hell isn't where I am walking down now
smoking the devil's lettuce
take me back to Lebanon so I can ask Jesus if I'll go to heaven
I'm too up

than I fall way, way down
I'll find myself in oblivion now\

/I remember the girl with the violet eyes looked at me
disappointingly
she said,
what are you running from
what thrill are you going to catch tonight\

/the city sucks you in
it suffocates you
with so much work to afford this rent
and then to go to work again
the next morning
it sucks you right in\

/I saw myself losing out on that future
which I promised myself
got caught up living a good life
having the man of my dreams love me
having money from three jobs
and no school to worry about

and free coke
I lived with my two best friends
a singer
and a drag queen
I kept chasing after the next adventure
every day had to be exciting
I couldn't be bored
I had to keep moving
but I wasn't focused on the right things\

/if you don't make time for your mental health
it will make time for you\

/I don't want to be blocked out anymore
by petty requests
that fill no woman's soul
like a desperate man trying to see me undressed
but I suppose
touch me like you do
for the time being
so I can feel something too
for the time being\

/loneliness will swallow you up
like a pack of cigarettes\

/sometimes you need to accept the fact
that not everything which affects your life
isn't solely based on affecting you
maybe it wasn't the best time for it to happen
but it could've been the right time for something else to align\

/I sat there
trying to hide my addiction from him
I was ashamed
when he was doing the same
just a different drug name\

/drugs either numb what you're hiding
or they amplify your pain\

/the pain of losing out on my future
the pain of being nothing
especially to the people who believed I would be nothing
I wanted to prove to them
almost more than myself
and that was half of the problem\

/every day I was working with people twenty years older than
    me
I was working in the kitchen
with cooks who've been pleading for decades to become chef's
I was working with professional photographers who begged to
    become famous for their work
I was walking dogs who's collars were more expensive than my
    apartment
and what was I?
a jack of many trades...
...a master of none\

/I promise I won't ever hurt you,
humans cannot promise things like this
after getting close to anyone
it's very easy to become sensitive

but be cautious
in the difference of paper cuts
to scars\

/one day,
while my coworker and I were prepping for dinner
he sighed,
I'm in trouble with my daughters middle school
why?
I asked
'cause I told her the truth about those famous fairytales,
he emphasized
see, that Goldilocks and The Three Bears is about a girl who ate one of
    those strong edibles
that she accidentally broke into a house
which she thought was her own
and being high,
Goldilocks had the munchies
so she ate all the food and then fell asleep in the most comfy bed
when the family came home she woke up
she was so high from that edible that she saw the family as bears
he said,
the moral of the story is don't eat an edible

then he told me about *The Princess and The Frog*
which was actually about STD's

that when the princess "kissed" (had sex with) the prince
he actually had worts on his you-know-what,
my coworker informed me
that's why he's depicted as a frog
so the princess turned into a frog too
being cursed forever with herpes

then he enlightened me about *Little Red Riding Hood*
that one's a lie too,
he expressed,
the wolf is a pedophile,
who stalks little girls and rapes them,
I nodded

so I told my 7 year old daughter this
and she decided to tell her whole class about rape, pedophiles
sex diseases
and edibles

apparently that's inappropriate talk
so now I gotta go down to her school and speak with the principle, be-
    cause the kids are apparently scarred from the real stories

I don't teach my kids lies,
they know Santa ain't real either
I'm not paying for all that shit and letting some old white man take the
    credit

/tell me how you properly make a body function
when the mind and heart
are in strenuous discomfort
that cannot be healed by anything except distracted time
or by him\

/I tried bargaining with the universe to give me more time
before all the good things came to a halt
though I needed to stop blaming others
reluctant to question myself
I have the power
waiting around begging and pleading for a miracle
when I could get up and do the labor\

/I knew
somewhere in me
that I had love for him
I would find myself incredibly happy over things not involving him
unconsciously I'd see him
thinking of how I wished I could share this happiness
I wanted him to be happy\

/I kept a lot to myself
I hid a lot from everybody else
should've been more careful
listened to those old folks
still
I continued to dabble\

/I wish you could love yourself
to see yourself in the way that I do
there is so much in you that deserves to be loved\

/I woke up
thinking of him
I went out with my friends
missing him
and I went home with another man
to fill the void
of wanting him
but even to distract myself with sex
is not enough to even attempt to diminish the fact
that long distance is so humanly hard to grasp
and that I finally wanted to dive into someone
but I still can't
because I am here

and he is somewhere else
out of my hands\

/he is as simply beautiful
as tripping acid
in the rain\

/I felt like we were just a group of stoners
dropped into another man's world\

I ask myself this so much—
/where would I be without my women?\

/we started before all of this
we are our culture
our race
our story

our ancestors
our history
do not forget where you came from\

/most *good* men became the way that they are
being surrounded by powerful women
and most of these strong women became so powerful because they
    were broken down by lesser men\

/somewhere
here
I've lost some of my passion
I want to gain it back
though I lack creativity
where there once was a garden of opportunity\

/oh, trust me
I have a heart
I just need to remember where I last lost it\

/I didn't feel the need to hide either of them
my neighbor was now my grown up neighbor
he moved two blocks away from me
and I trusted my California man\

/love is so strange to me
it's funny
you can spend time with a person every day and without knowing
    grow to love them
it's natural
look at all your friends who've stayed for so long
look at your annoying coworker you've worked with for years
there's something about each of them that you love so much, and
    there's dumb shit they do that's irritating as hell, but still you
    love them\

/but I blame movies
I blame my dad for teaching me life through movies and TV shows
they know exactly how to take a bad man, keep him going, make
    him evil, so much so that you hate him with your own passion,
    and slowly turn the anti hero into the hero
but he isn't perfect, he does something fucked up, and we can relate
    almost so because we are human, but the audience saw how

much he grew, watched his character development
and yet, they still have some sort of hope, we still keep watching
I used to think I was brilliant when it came to predicting people
but when you get too close it becomes so difficult to see the worst
your brain can't imagine betrayal
I've thought of this, and I'd choose loyalty over love
real loyalty
you can be loyal to someone without loving them
but you can love someone and still betray them
how fucked is that?\

/I'm trying to get through the things that I don't talk about\

/I want to build you up
all collective community
I am extremely happy for my friends success
if I'm eating
we're all eating\

/and I found myself some days
fabricating the truth to make myself seem more presentable
in order to impress him
because while he was still human, he appeared perfect

maybe another mans trash is a girls treasure boy
and I wanted to shine like diamonds
whenever I were near him
sometimes those diamonds were cubic zirconia
he found them sparkly anyhow
and at the time
to me,
that's what counts

/at the age of my adolescence
I wanted to hold up that silver spoon to feed my parents
more wealth than they could've given to me
from him being the product of an immigrant father
and her mother sailing in from Italy
they clothed us with sturdy love and my mom did what she could
    to keep us warm
in her rough arms
I wanted to give them a better life than they gave me

I wanted to shower them in gold and honey
it was my turn to keep them warm\

/sometimes in life we have to accept
that we can be on the lighted path
while other times we're traveling through dark tunnels\

/even though we were lakes and oceans apart
sometimes I could still feel his hand on my arm
telling me he'd hold me soon\

/I learned I had to let go to heal
I had to keep walking to make it to tomorrow
it's difficult letting go when you haven't finished the game\

/put yourself out there
have some fun
it's better than staying inside\

/we as humans like to stay in our comfort zone\

/to escape the void of this intimidating tower
of loneliness I've seemed to uphold
attempting to climb down this spiral staircase with hands full
I've drank down the bottle of depression and isolation
neglected to look for help
as our tower burns there
in crimson flames
I see it crumble with remains
maybe I'll leave faster that way

/I had my man
though he was so far away from where I stand
I still recall when he held my hand
and that was good enough for the time being
while I miss his being
he leaves me full
though at the end of the day I am drained
out of useless energy
that could've been spent filling my soul with my craft
my passion that burns my hands when I don't use it
seems to lack
in and out with breaths
I don't have the courage to fail
so I don't try to win
I forfeit the game
hide my shame

of not winning at fame
seems to drift
in and out of oblivion
wash out
there remains of my sins
vanishes in the violet flames
left of him
we float back
in and out of love again\

/the girl with the violet eyes
asked me where I'd been for some time

I lost myself miles and miles down that cheap road
full of drugs and numbing myself
could not find my way home
I kept it from him
felt shame for the things I had done\

/I suppose I am somewhere between
searching for lost clarity
and accepting the fact that I won't receive all the answers to my
    grief\

/*boom*
boom
crash
she takes her nose to 7 deadly souls
lines on lines she goes
tumbling down in her stilettos
running around with those other hoes
who she just met two days ago
kept it clean
keep it kosher
singing,
we run this dojo,
let em know,
we don't take invitations
we give out the business
mind your P's n' Q's
it's just how we do
catch this beat
acting like we're billionaires from Wall Street
like we're old enough to take this heat
watch your feet
you can't see what you can't seek\

/feeling lonely
while being loved

by many
is a desperately sad place to be in\

/she wished she could function better on these drugs\

/eager is the fox coming out to play
dreams sweeping far away
nestled in the corner is another romance hunter
looking for his bounty
love leads the lonely
tired of theses stained tears left on my borrowed body\

/be courteous to your feelings
be gentle as you guide yourself through life
be kinder to your body
be awakened to your knowledge\

/I found that the next morning
these drugs made me sadder than what I was hiding from\

/you called me while you were tripping
because you said you missed me
that has to mean something\

/my dreams gnawed at my heels
waking me from endless worry
my restless nights would catch me if my Saturday night fever
     didn't\

/be verbal in what you want
it may be obvious to you what you want
but it could be much simpler if you verbalized what you need from
     your partner\

/I know you're hurting
a thousand swords to your chest
every time you lay in bed to think about the things you cannot
      speak on yet
and I know you need someone to say, how they love you through all
      of this suffering and I wish I could be the one to love you
though we both know I can't
but I'll love you in my heart
I just don't have the heart to tell you that\

/they talk of time being the ultimate healer
but time only drifts it further and further from your day to day life
it's still there in other aspects
I believe every human carries the past with them
and you should
you need to stay with these things you've gone through to use as
      motivation to better your future and to be more aware that
      those things will not happen again\

/you're in-charge of your mindset
don't let them convince you otherwise\

/there's a fine line
of telling too much
yet saying not enough\

/for the time being
I was stuck in being a shell of a person\

/you can still love the person
and not agree with some of their opinions\

/talk is cheap
actions are expensive\

/I need to remind myself of how I can be a healer
but I cannot fix people
even though I desperately want to fix so many people
I want to shower them with roses
with vibrant colors

BLOOD ORANGE

I am a lover
I am a lover
and I want them to feel this love too\

/you know when you can trust someone
you can feel it
you can feel that you can trust them
and he was someone whom I could trust\

/you told me things that I know you couldn't tell your homies\

/I am here to love, but I ain't no damn sucker\

/he told me to stay away from that white girl powder
while he was slinging O's\

/a lot of judgment
comes from jealousy\

/I am someone who enjoys having a consistent routine
I yearn to be comfortable in all aspects of my life
this has been something that I've struggled with due to my anxiety
    and trust issues these things hold me back from living more
    free
I stay with consistent friends, consistent TV shows, consistent
    wines, consistent authors, consistent restaurants, consistent
    clothing stores, consistent jobs, consistent vacations
though through time I've gained a different perspective of myself
    and others when being put into elements I am not familiar
    with
our generation is the expert on making everybody feel comfortable
    that we tremble at the seams when put into situations we don't
    feel secure about
I suppose that can be one case of how our generation is so quick to
    judge others based on politics, based on race, location, religion,
    background, class, certain career paths
because we don't allow ourselves to know the other side
we have preconceived notions and we stick to them as if they don't
    bend
we stay in what we can mostly relate to
that much of our world is separated based off of not feeling com-
    fortable

I've known this about myself and it is something I used to really
    struggle with
especially being around people who have a different view on the
    world than you do
since moving to Chicago, I've forced myself to be in uncomfortable
    situations which have tested me in ways I've never endured
either way it's made me into a stronger woman, and it's educated
    me, and given me more of an open mind
unfortunately our generation as Americans we flaunt as if we are
    open minded, that we include everybody, we want everyone
    to feel comfortable, but truly we aren't inclusive and we aren't
    open minded beyond what we deem is politically correct
there's three sides of the spectrum
there are people who support Trump
people who support Hilary
and the people who don't support either, but they decide which is
    the lesser of two evils
it's been uncomfortable and difficult having someone very close to
    me support our president
striking back and defending him
until there's nothing left but disagreeing the others side
I found that there is no black and white, no easy way, no one per-
    son to fix this
but dealing with somebody who I shall not name defending a man
    I do not support
it is heartbreaking
though it makes me realize we have to love each other for the con-
    tent of our character
to put aside our differences and focus on improving and having an

KABDO

open mindset
and allowing somebody to tap into your world and maybe under-
stand
and you can do the same
we won't learn anything much of what we do not know when we
stay in what makes us oh so comfortable
get uncomfortable
see what you find\

/I tried loving once, didn't enjoy the aftertaste\

/he thought of me
while he took those drugs\

/exhausted from the heat of the kitchen
exhausted from these cut drugs setting in
exhausted from my man being disappointed in my after work plans
exhausted from being sober
exhausted from my work taking over

exhausted from my man not buying a plane ticket to come and see
    me\

/found myself here for the time being
champagne taste
while on a beer budget\

/you'll find me here most nights
slipping away
but not to the point to where I've vanished

though I'm never here entirely anymore
and I've grown accustom to numbing my resentment

he asked me to be vulnerable for once,

have I found a coward
or an angel in the violet hour?

9. A normal girl

/when I stopped fiending for a thrill
the world became so much more clear
and yet I understand why they fiended for the yayo
as they do so\

/I missed him so much
and I wondered why God put us together
was this supposed to be a torturous love affair?
why wasn't he here?
I missed him so much my eyes cried out real tears
my heart was so far away from his\

/good things come to those who hustle\

/to whom much is given much is tested
but to whom little of much is given even more is tested\

/stepped inside to find you here again
we met where the climate was so warm
near you
like two wolves who hadn't seen each other in years\

/I never want to leave,
you said to me,
let's stay here for a little while longer,
and you held me there
while you ran your fingers through my hair
you kissed my forehead
as my stomach filled with vibrating butterflies bombing to be let
    out of their cage
and around our heads like halos
you swayed me back and forth like Ray Charles
was humming us to sleep
I felt the warmth of your heart through your T-shirt
your energy told me what you didn't have to show\

/I remember the day the world went silent
and it was spent with me in your arms\

/spending the days with him
was like those old times at Disney World like Christmas morning
    as a child
it was like spending the day with a movie star
I felt so special
he was mine
and I was his
I felt so lucky to be loved by him\

/no other soul mattered
all that was on my mind was loving you
holding you
kissing you
wrapping myself up in you
I remember we laid in that motel bed all day
not to have sex
just to hold each other
I'd never felt somebodies love for me
like that
besides my mother\

/you kissed my hand
while it was entangled in yours

and you said,
if I could end my days with you
I'd fall back in love every morning

/we spent our 21st birthdays
wrapped up in each other
with a legally bought bottle of Crown on the vintage coffee table
and a purled legal blunt laying on the cleaned ash tray\

/two taurus'
two wolves
two alien's in love\

/I blame Hollywood
for why I am attracted to broken men
they make these underdogs seem so desirable\

/when he relayed the traumas
he's been through
all I could imagine was him as a child
as a high schooler
I wished I could've been there
to be there for him
I would've been there in a heartbeat for him\

/every touch of you echoed
it escaped like small breaths from a baby
trying to find the words to articulate this
but all I could find was magic
dusted in my palms to the edge of my finger tips
then I came back to reality
found myself here for the time being
wished time could stop for you and I to be
it lingered a little
moved too swiftly
and you vanished in the flames
I still feel your arms around my shoulders
holding me up with your Phoenix wings
sailed me through your deep dreams
keep a piece of me here with you
I will be your echoing muse\

/I could feel it
burned in with crimson
blood orange oozed within him
bleeding red
find us dead
entangled in each other's web
love steamed
making marks on our windows\

/California and him
was a perfect
and yet a deadly combination\

/I want you to focus on being your most authentic self
whatever that may be
learn that you need to accept yourself before you can achieve that
    acceptance from others
I want you to focus on being nonjudgmental towards your peers
you cannot teach what you haven't learned, and you cannot learn
    what you haven't been taught
many times you may not want to be the teacher, sometimes people
    need to be taught what they haven't learned yet
I want you to focus on momentum
of what gives you true momentum, what moves you in your daily
    life
I want you to focus on what is toxic in your life and how you can

pull it out
root and stem
sometimes, as people, we crave that drama
we like to be reminded that we hold some sort of sparked emotion
    in someone else's life
we are sometimes too insecure to properly articulate how we need
    verbal reassurance
verbal recognition
instead we take the path of manipulation
those are toxic traits we need to sort out
as a generation we need to learn how to communicate our emo-
    tions in a healthier way
and we need to stop comparing ourselves
we're different for a fucking reason
use that to your advantage\

/he told me
of how he didn't want to be a limitation in my life
and I said,
I want you in my life
he said,
good,
because I want you to stay here

/my heart submerges me into troubled waters
of love that can't breathe for far too long underneath the surface
and yet I come up
coughing out old tunes of unexpressed love that I stored as grief
    years ago
I've learned how to love myself when nobody cared to see me
    swim\

/nature is so beautiful
we can obtain much knowledge of our world by studying the laws
    of nature
trees grow by splitting themselves in half
they create beautiful extensions of themselves that end up shedding
    season after season
as new life grows back
they're rooted to the earth
there are humans
and there are people
humans are our innate form
people are far more complicated
when we add imagination and emotion
at the end
we are rooted from the earth too\

/it is not vain to love thy self \

/I am my harshest critic
I am my most brave soldier
I am my most bold cheerleader
I am a journey
I am a work in progress\

/laying my head on his muscular chest
to feel his breath
up and down
slowly
the calm of the morning ocean rising and falling
as she wades on her surf board
waiting to ride him all over again\

/tomorrow is not promised
but I can promise you this

you're in charge of your own narrative
make it a damn story you want to read\

/*you get what you give out*
manifest love and positive energy into your life
breathe out supportive affection
lift others up
share what you have
give, give, give
recognize what your aura is and how you present that to the world
understand your background
your culture
give love
we need more love in this world
I want CNN to show me some love\

/in the city
you age fast
or you die young\

/I could sit here in silence with you for so long
time is irrelevant when I am in your arms\
/I am attempting to be more vulnerable
it's difficult when my words have been weaponized against me
I see blood orange when I trust somebody
a rare color
I am learning to be more honest with my emotions
life isn't as complicated when you're straight forward\

/understand your boundaries with toxic people
life happens
sometimes people cant be there for you the way you are for them
that's okay, but make sure the value is there

you're worthy of being valued
plus tax
understand the difference between narcissism and taking care of
    yourself
narcissists are usually verbally manipulative
typically they'll gaslight you when their being questioned, and they
    aren't necessarily very giving to others, but they will take
narcissists tend to deflect any criticism that comes their way
taking care of yourself could look like: they'll pass on hanging out
    because they can't financially afford it
or them being honest when you don't agree with it
humans at the end of the day are selfish creatures
and I think all of us should help others as long as thyself is taken
    care of\

/there is compromise in relationships
that goes for friendships and sexual relationships
if there isn't a give and take
than that's a one way relationship\

/the person I love the most is my mom
and he had a similar spirit to hers
it drew me closer to him for it

one day I won't have her to hold me down
I wanted someone else with a love able spirit\

/I asked him,
what?
I just like looking at you is all,
he replied\

/I could divulge my words to him
like he just fried up
some honey, butter chicken
and I decorated the cream pie
letting my past get him locked in it
for a little while
sympathizing with me
letting my words simmer there on his tongue
while he soothed my back
kissed my neck
cradled me in his arms
I could feel how warm he was
I felt so safe here\

/I could still smell your cologne
on my motel pillowcase\
/why do I always seem to cry on airplanes?\

/leaving him in that desert
again
was one of the hardest goodbyes I've had to give\

/if my two coworkers
could've been married to each other for 8 years
have three kids together
go through divorce
and work on the line during dinner rushes 6 days out of the week
    together
than I can get through today\

/anxious people
love anxious distractions\

/my girls and I rode through the city
counting the stars on our freckled backs
making maps of our future
trying to connect the dots to our success
leaving tracks behind our mess\

/be careful
we're all human
you never know someone fully\

/I'll wear my red dress for the show,
a lilac penciled in drawing
swinging back and forth over your dashboard
with my name on the ink signing
Mississippi Half Step Uptown Toodeloo on the station

he rolls up one,
we spark up the conversation

cherry red, Pepsi Cola, melanin dipped in his skin, smoked weed
    since his pre-teens, deadhead fan,
a hippie loving, republican
something doesn't seem to match

mom reminds me that we all have our vices

keep me kept up in your spice cabinet
jars stuffed with notes you've never sent
Mikey Mouse from Romero you left on your childhood desk
parting gifts your father wished you had

paintings from past experiences
she holds them up to the light, it reflects in turquoise pigments
so cloud headed he can't see what's beyond the surface
keep my mind medicated
call that marijuana service

and at Mississippi River bonfires,
he tries to keep me warm,
though I know he's still with her

though who could forget, mama loves chocolate turtles and Louie's
      kisses
she adores modern vintage
cruising in your 1992 cabriolet convertible with Charlemagne and
      Susan
and she can't hate
though she's in a steady disillusion
she thinks I remind her of what she's losing\

/notice your worth
look at your surroundings
what do I have to be thankful for?

we take so many things for granted that we neglect appreciation
everything is temporary
take the moment to appreciate five things
then think of losing those five things\

/I wasn't left worrying about him
I felt confident
I felt loved
I felt full
both of us hungry for money and success
in our opposing futures
we wanted to lift each other up to the highest peak
and yet
he was not here to share in our milk and honey\

/if you assumed I wasn't being charged interest for my bad karma
you were wrong\

/be with someone who excites you
who makes you a little nervous\

/everything seems to come back full circle
she calls in the full moon to save me
coming back up like the sun took the day off
left me on the night shift
kept me counting the stars like Atticus
kept me leading the pack
like the wolf I am
kept me walking but not telling me when it'll end
leave me to wander
I am who I am\

my girls lullaby-

/I wear my heart on my sleeve for you all
you're my hand that leads me to a better path
you're my guided mediation
that I don't need to ask
you play me a tune on the sax
give me some love some inspiration
dive into the good vibrations
you know me better than anybody else
you hear me when I don't listen to myself\

/spent my days sleeping in
thinking of him holding me
I spent my afternoons slaving away in the kitchen
dreaming of making it
spent my nights with my girlfriends
eating spaghetti and drinking champagne from red solo cups\

/you cannot run from your energy
it will turn up within people you did not expect
being deceitful
will manifest deceitful people in your surroundings
if you lie
you'll be matched with liars
you attract what you project\

/many suffer because of their egos
it is difficult to obtain knowledge when you're struggling from an
    ego death experience
see beyond yourself \

/wake up earlier
get shit done
be productive
get a job
smoke some pot
sage that room
you'll feel better\

/I had a big family in Chicago

my pops was an old man from the Odyssey
told me of stories to infinity
he taught me lessons us kids should've learned at a younger age

my bigger brother was my coworker
taught me about love and so forth
taught me how to be loyal when you got nothing left but sorrow
and some chum change in your pockets to go

my uncle was Tory
told me stories of his glory
and how his old girl almost got him killed
he survived so much
though he never died
he died a little inside
he never lies

I could trust that they had my back
because they've caught me
in the times where I have fallen\

/men don't get buttaflies, they get moths mate\

/cubic zirconia
look at who's fooling ya
don't got drugs on you?
then beat it up like I'm teaching salsa

love you, slow motion rider
like jerk chicken fire
ocean drive
girls weekend
tattoo vibe
your boy's tweakin'
porch light left on
cigarette resting in Autumn's hand now it's gone
don't wait for this love to catch you
I'm making memories behind the scenes without you\

/I think depending on how messy my room is
depends on how messy my life is\

/talking about my duel drunken personalities,
I know slut and whore made an appearance\

/being too numb
too much of the time\

/I went to sleep with him
my neighbor
my old friend
on that same, vintage bed we used to sleep in
with his moms knitted blanket
he held me
only a little
and we both fell asleep there
with his chin in the crook of my neck\

/speaking it into existence\

/I don't have a dimmer
I'm either on
or I'm off\

/if I cannot submerge my whole heart into it
than I don't want it\
/when I am at work
I put my heart and soul into it
I give them my energy and focus
because everything I do
wether it's at work or walking down Michigan Avenue
I am representing myself
I want to bring my best work to the table\

/I may be a slow learner at certain things
but I learn
eventually\

/it's funny
you'll watch females forgive men for the pettiest circumstances
but they won't forget the smallest things you've done\

/I love my women
but damn
sometimes we'll be so snooty for the wrong reasons
some girls just won't like you simply because you're pretty
and that's a fact\

/I love when my guy friends interrupt the dude who just interrupt-
    ed me
to say,
but Carmen, what were you saying?
because as women
we get cut off so much that it's appreciative to hear of men
wanting their women to be heard\

/my neighbor and I went on an adventure
we climbed through tunnels and trees
over fences

with colorful graffiti
he takes pictures of me\

/culture is so fascinating to me
we were sculpted so long ago
by the blood
sweat and cold tears
of our hardworking ancestors
who've paved a path
of tired success
for us to walk here
to form a modern day life
reminding ourselves that these souls
reflect our culture
as we continue down a path
of which our ancestors molded in an attempt
for us to succeed\

/I cannot trust a stingy b*tch
just a rule of thumb\

/I am Italian and Arab
and a cook
so when I walk into a Whole Foods
it's like
a virgin
walking into a Japanese whorehouse
on
cocaine\

/take me at the moment\

/I was villainized for moving on\

/you may not have to experience it to understand it
but you have to go through it to feel it\

/*I miss this place,*
I mumbled
this place misses you,
he said\

10. a girl tries to forget

/there is a strict process
of holding on
and letting go
many don't know the balance
many crash
and the things they're holding don't break the fall\

/I tried to forget
shut my eyes a thousand times
it never diminishes entirely
still
like grey ashes falling
looking like snow drifting
mistake it for beauty
when it was once deadly\

/some days I felt like I was trapped in a glass case
don't knock on the walls
they'll shatter and break\

/y'all man
will be too horny and miss out on a real home girl\

/it's true
I have guy friends
I have best friends who're guys
yes the majority of them would sleep with me

but they know what's up and that it's not going to happen
so that sexual stuff isn't a problem\

/moving too fast
juggling what I don't have
coming up with white powder\

/souls travel together
this is not my first life on this planet
but I am confident that it is my last\

/I've always been such a nonjudgmental soul
who am I to judge?
if you have not sinned than throw the first stone

we need to uplift more often the characters who're living a life
that is not a sis, white life
uplift people of color
transgender women and men
non-binary folks
in fact all of the LGBTQ
I am so proud of you all\

/I was trying desperately
to get through life
without talking about the rough moments
that left me feeling naked
which seems to be inescapable\

/my body knew before my mind
that this was another part of my trauma
my body tensed
before my mind could catch up to the signs
seeing people like him, was apart of my sexual trauma
I could not hide from it\

/the body will tell you before the mind does\

/I am depleted
from my aggravating mental health
seeping like fog into my pores
smoking me out
breathing in toxins that manifest as aliens

BLOOD ORANGE

in the bleak, night sky
I feel worn out from fighting this anxiety
mental health makes me want to lay in bed all day
waking up is so exhausting\

/fighting to stay awake\

/don't need a therapist
I go to my psychic
get my palm read by a bad b*tch
she blames it on the stars huh
I blame it on the road I walk with my feet
bruising my heart\

/spending all this time with dreamers
of older people, of people my age
pleading for success
makes a wolf anxious
of not achieving this point
defaulting to an average life
never making it to the joint

failure to launch the action
will land in nothingness
we all wanted to make it
and I knew
we weren't all going to make it\

/I remember that moment
of working so hard at my photography job
I got promoted\

/but at the end of it all
I wanted to be surrounded by him
because he made me laugh\

/I find that when I see something that makes me happy
I think of my mom
that I want to share this happiness with her\

/she came to me at night
unexpectedly
drowning in complete and empty sadness
I'd never seen on her like this
she was seeking my comfort
to heal her in that moment
she trusted no one else
saying to me
why, why?
begging to ask herself
why aren't I good enough?
her tears left pink stained lines
roaming down her unwelcome cold checks

in that moment
I had never felt I had so much love inside me
so I gave her everything I could
she kept asking me,
why aren't I good enough?
I held her shoulders up
as I did, I began to cry too
and I told her she was everything to me and gave me everything
        she had
it was my turn to be strong
it was my time to give it back
all that I had
I steadied her body from shaking down
as she wept like a lonely weeping willow
but I was there to hear her sounds

it is quiet interesting
a different outlook on life
when a mother falls apart in her daughters arms

I often saw my mother as this embodiment of something so
    grounded and unbreakable
she sacrificed her whole life to raise us
and yet
I've hardly seen any cracks in her
and out of all my friends
my mother is my most valuable armor
she has protected me through everything which I couldn't have
    fought off on my own

and when I saw her shatter
that sadness I had felt
I let myself hold onto

I realized how loving someone is
the closest thing we have to magic\
/we as women
put this colossal pressure on ourselves to be desired
we're chugging that kool-aid every fuckin' morning
the standard of a woman's body
comparing ourselves to models we've never seen in person
buying into these girls who sell poisoned drinks to make us skinnier
we're supposed to be a size 2
with big boobs and a fat ass
we spend all this money on plastic surgery

and for what?
what standard do men have to achieve?\

/*we'll go back to that motel someday,*
you said to me
over the phone\

/if I've learned some things
it's take the medication as prescribed\

/we shame women for being too beautiful
we shame women for not being attractive enough
we shame women for being as sexually active as society deems okay
    for men
yet we shame women for not being sexual enough for a man
we shame women for being less intelligent
yet we shame women for being "know it alls"
we're damned if we do and damned if we don't
I told you it was a fine line to walk across\

/it's quite sad
how we see other peoples success
as our failures\

/he wanted me to be the shadow
of the perfect person he wanted himself to be with\

/instead of being the truthful boyfriend
he wanted to play the role of being the hypocritical father\

/I shed fear
like snake skin
I hold fear like I'm hugging satan
no rest for the wicked
got a lot of baggage but none of these are designer luggage\

/there is immense amounts of love stored in you to be cherished

don't forget your talents
your passions
love yourself till the world can feel it
nobody else fights like you\

/I came back to my Chicago apartment
eucalyptus in an old pinto grigio bottle
with condoms and Coco Chanel on the coffee table
I like to pick and choose
J Cole in my headphones
I live above a coffee shop
that's the perk of a misread millennial
driving downtown
late to work as usual
dressed in my chef coat
as usual
speed walking across navy pier
8 hour shift here

the battery drained in my headphones
but I'm still kicking it
I spot Donny Woz down the block, asking me for a cigarette
hollering,
I need me a damn cigarette,
but that's just some Chicago shit\

/hear we go again
playing the jealous boy
where does the lack of trust come from?\

/just 'cause I look cute doesn't make me a hoe\

/just because other men find me attractive does not make me a
    hoe\

/just because I like the attention, that does not make me a hoe\

/because I have bigger boobs and a small waist and thick thighs,
    my body type does not make me a hoe\

/I knew he wasn't with other girls
so why was he so convinced I was with other men?\

/was in the mood
horny for love\

/didn't know in the moment
how complicated you felt about the situation
didn't know it had you twisted
had to find out by twitter that you're mad about this shit
mad at the decision
to make this an open relationship
I have felt the fire
and I adore the embers
let it transpire
but I still have to guard my heart
like lava rocks
setting up metal blocks
making sure you can't get past these guards
didn't know in the moment
you didn't show it
kept it pushing
and still we keep floatin'\

/he said over the phone,
I trust you...
I just don't trust them\

/fresh orchids
baby, I'm the florist
come to my garden
sip on some cold coffee with the locals
toke on this doobie just to show 'em
tell me of your worries
I'll listen\

/after a while
a mango will become very delicate
even if well preserved
if it's alone and never touched
it can still bruise
and it can bruise just as easy if held in gentle hands\

/okay, I admit
I'm happier
when I'm tan
and in a mid wine drunk laugh\

/the most important art project
you can create
is significantly crucial
it is heart wrenching
it is loving
it is soothing
it is breaking
it is tiring
it is beautiful
it is sacrificing
it is a life time
of molding
and crumbling
and layers
and processing
and full exposure
when you create yourself
that should be your most worthy project\

/a lot of the times
I don't like to make myself
personally vulnerable
to anyone\

/I came to the neighbor
for advice about long distance relationships
he gave me a few tips
though he relayed of how hard it is\

/the fighter always wins\

/be your own person first\

/I remember how Tory told me,
if you can't do it for yourself,
than do it for your mama\

/men will be worried
when they know they have a good one
'cause they know other men can see it too\
/many people are afraid of the truth\

/I'm a girls girl
however, I love my boys
'cause there's never drama or sensitivity
I can give them shit and they'll give it right back\

/*try to look through my lens once*,
I told the girl with the violet eyes,
if you moved to Chicago you'd see the world differently
my eyes have witnessed multitudes of things in Chicago
that I wouldn't have seen anywhere else
other than on TV\

/all I know is you have to make room for yourself
no ones here to save your spot\

/I wished I would've let him in on how much I adored him
maybe I was dishonest about my feelings
kept them close to my chest
I didn't want him to know the power he had\

/I woke up in the middle of the night
to my heart screaming with anguish
I tried swallowing its heavy pain for awhile
but my heart lathered me in such potent sadness
it was stronger than me
my heart seemed to be sobbing for quite some time
and I was becoming conscious of its tears
I could not ignore it now
I knew exactly what it was searching for
what it was begging me to find
bleeding through my stomach
with shoe string tears
knotted up tight in my body
my heart wept for his
but he was so far away from here
as it continued to scream
I didn't know how to keep my heart from romancing this pain
yelling at me to fix this emptiness
I said,
try not to feel it
but my heart knew that I couldn't

so it begged still
pleading on in relentless guilt
beating louder and louder
like the echoing rhyme of a southern drum
before another heart wrenching war has begun
it jabbed at me
all night
restless and stubborn
until I saw the pink sky
melting the darkness away
I suppose
I had missed him so much
that my body woke me up
crying
bleeding red for him
and I never knew until then
how missing someone could affect my heart to this extent\

/there was magic
in being loved by him\

/be with somebody who makes you excited to wake up
someone who showers you in rainbows so that you can swim in
    color
someone who knows your boundaries

who lifts you towards the sun
someone who makes you feel like you're the only one\

/I didn't need to be told
I could feel it\

/my mental health was so draining
some mornings I'd struggle to just get out of bed
I felt as though I had no purpose\

/I feel this immense pressure to be somebody
somebody of importance
that my voice matters
I don't know why
and yet it doesn't matter
we are all in our very own simulation
find that balance within yourself
spend time unlearning self hate
push yourself to be better
tell yourself it's going to be better if I make it better\

/I liked to be reminded that he was still here\

/I always make the wrong decisions
when I dabble with her\

/jealousy breeds animosity\

/I wasn't doing anything with these other men
but sometimes he needed to be reminded that I could\

/I suppose I wasn't all that innocent in his jealousy\

/two years was spent with him
I would come to really fucking miss his energy

like withdrawing from nicotine
it burns slowly
through my lingerie
feeling lonely
touch myself for the time being
play with that bunny
I ain't no playboy bunny
but I'll sure pose for Mr. Money
spiraling down the rabbit hole
just to ring in the milk n' honey\

/when your best friend has been best friends with your man since
    they were children\

/get out of your comfortable zone
especially if you're privileged
recognize that others are less fortunate and live a life of less choices
make an effort to educate yourself on other cultures besides your
    own
take time to give back to those communities that are struggling
notice the communities who're being gentrified
there are plenty of neighborhoods in Chicago that are experiencing
    gentrification
prices continue to rise in poorer communities
it pushes the hard-working, lower class further and further away
    from the city

forcing the citizens into even more dangerous areas
be aware
listen and learn to things that aren't necessarily directly apparent to
    you\

/the negative affect on an empath is attracting toxic people\

/things that are good memories for the soul
walking along the ocean by myself
driving around the river road listening to Time by Pink Floyd
staying in Sam's boathouse docked at Beer Can Island
listening to Jay screaming the song Caroline in my ear
writing at Spyhouse coffee shop
walking to the light house with my neighbor and seeing the city
    skyline while we drink a beer
ordering Harold's with Alonzo and watching When Harry Met
    Sally before the Patriots won the super Bowl
making Lebanese food for my friends
playing with puppies and kittens drunk
or sober
being in a foreign country
the moment you both realize *this is good sex*
snorkeling in Maui

is like discovering Atlantis
when someone goes out of their way to show that they care
watching Entourage and drawing
listening to my grandparents tell their stories
going to Lily's cabin with Greta and Connor
laughing with friends\

/I understood
why he couldn't trust me\

/he was tired of hearing about the other, dull boys
if he had really listened
he would've known
they had nothing on him\

/make my baby some homemade supper
let him light the sky up with this old lover
bleeding violet
for the time we've become awaken to it
love you long time

till the sun comes up in your time zone
let the world know
how I love you so\

/I knew he was jealous
I knew he was worried
but I wasn't doing anything with anybody else
he just didn't trust me
and that made me more angry
because I only wanted him\

/I had to learn how to read
passive aggressiveness
because it wasn't in my dictionary\

/I went out with my coworkers for a Halloween party
we got a little too wasted
blow was involved
that was the first mistake\

/I told my California man I'd be out at my coworkers party
and the tone of the text was not pleasing
we got into a small argument of him thinking my boss wanted to
    sleep with me
solely because I told him my boss and I were going out to smoke
    before the party\

/make me feel like a hoe than I'll bring out the real hoe
that you don't want to see\

/I wish we could've communicated our boundaries better
he didn't let me know how he felt till it was too late\

/there were precautions I should've taken to not let him worry so
    much about me\

/apart of me selfishly liked the emotion it would provoke from him
but I would never let him know that\

/the whole night was a dazed blur
spent it swinging around dancing and slinging drinks
let my Lebanese dancing back into my life
show my coworkers too much of a good time
beaming till the sun came up
snorting snow till the sun came up
chatting with friends till the sun came up

next thing I knew
I was alone with my coworker\

/*that shouldn't have happened,*
I exhaled, as he was still on top of me,
you need to go\

/the sun rose
no sleep was obtained

knots in my stomach tightened
as I stared at my naked mistake\

/the second it went in
I knew I had fucked up\

/I avoided him all day
couldn't even talk to him regularly
without feeling insufferable pain
seeping so heavy
I fucked up
badly\

/and the next day
I received more karma
come knock on my door\

/don't use sex to validate your beauty
you'll usually end up feeling uglier than you did before\

/even though he never called me those derogatory names,
I still felt the shame
it was an unjust verdict
from an over thinking, anxious man
which made me want to lash out
and give him what he was manifesting in me to be
what he feared I would become\

/I suppose in wanting him
or wanting validation because I lacked receiving that from him
selfishly I made a crucial mistake
though I tried convincing myself that we made the decision to be
    in an open relationship
even though we agreed
no coworkers... or friends...\
/I wanted to be adored
I wanted to be put on that diamond spinning pedestal
I wanted to be felt up and down like fine leather
I wanted to be desired

I wanted to feel sexy like Marilyn
and I wanted to be the greatest thrill your life has ever been\

/I already knew what he was going to say
so there was no sense in telling him what really happened\

/we were in an open relationship,
I recited to myself in a whisper
over and over again
but still I could not bring myself to tell him\

/we make these choices
we eat and drink the venom
that we've served up for ourselves
and then we are astonished
when we feel so ill after it all\

/I felt so empty
I needed to be filled up with you
but I didn't have the heart to communicate the situation\

12 miles of separation–

/I remember that day you called,
the hint of anxiousness was felt
your voice bubbling up
worried
you could feel my hesitation
with you waiting
to know why I was so distant
leaving you speechless
but I gave no information
just a false explanation\

/he knew something was up
he zig-zagged his way to ask if I had slept with my boss and was
    that why I'd been so distant
I said I didn't sleep with my boss
and kept the conversation steered towards a whole other direction
if I don't talk about the party

than I don't have to lie\

/you knew how to read me\

/why is the truth so painful
when the lies seem so pleasurable
when the the truth is hurtful
lies become entangled

got a web around the joint
the crib cant hear the noise
twelve got a call around the corner
they'll be coming around sooner
no fair warning to these loiters

coming back up just to hurt you
where the truth is
you lost it with your bruises
choosing
not to see too much pain
coming back up just to feed you
coming back up just to feel you
why is the truth so painful

when the lies seem so entangled\

/he knew he knew he knew
but he didn't know for sure\

/I don't want to be fucked
I want to be desired dammit\

/I went looking for validation
in the wrong places\

/my abandonment issues
will hold me down
like my demon I see in my sleep paralysis\

/try as hard as you can to always be honest
to tell the truth
if you lie often you'll attract liars
I can attest to this statement\

/the girl with the violet eyes
told me to be truthful
but there was so much I didn't know how to tell him\

/pain is insufferable
it is humans who tire out
keep walking\

the one who trained dragonflies-

/I love my grandmother
she fills me with love and desire
trust and faith
she knows no hate
compares to no other

kind hearted
a hardworking woman
how I aspire to love in the way that she does\

/everything we do translates to art
my suffering is art
when I cook for my love that is art
how I tell a story is art
the way I love is art
how I stand up for others is art
my body is art
the way I see myself is art\

/cooks in the kitchen
are a different type of asshole\

/I don't know what is worse?
lying to your boyfriend about sort of cheating on him
or not being able to get away from the guy you cheated with?
he didn't understand that after the incident

we couldn't be friends like that
he had to be cut off
I was fine with that
except he was my coworker\

/I had ambitions
that would someday make my grandmother proud\

/he told me I reminded him of home
I felt like I had left the door open
when I promised to keep the home safe\

/I knew the stigma hadn't faded yet\

/the economy markets off of selling sex
selling sexy women on the front covers that you read on your gold-
    en toilets

yet we shame women for being naked
we shame women for selling their bodies to make a profit for
    themselves
when the industry profits off of selling sexwork\

/lies never work out
most of the time they get exposed\

/you took acid and called me
I took acid and thought of my day dreams
becoming a reality
seeing it in fine print
in the daily
magazines weekly\

/we have the ability to create life
a woman is the closest thing to God\

/don't just focus on spreading more love
to make change
focus on educating yourself on how to change
putting in the effort and the time
outside of social media to help
put your blood sweat and tears into this
hold yourself accountable
reflect on your past actions
so much is from ignorance
ignorance is such a stained word
but truly, we cannot learn what we haven't been taught and we can't
     teach what we haven't learned
so do your part to teach yourself what you've lacked to learn
we can learn to be more mindful
we need to put forth the effort at first
your intentions are important
but real progress is action\

/like Batman and Robin
you can't catch me
I'm too swift for these lame babies
wanna cry on the daily
getting mixed up in dramas
that never matched up with y'all
wanna go toe to toe with us
we just laugh it off\

/I remember when the pain was too heavy
I had to console with Tory
he told me,
go to your mom
she'll know just where to fix it

/good to see my mom again
my old companion
I tell her things that other people don't know of
I tell her what's been bothering me and then some
she consoles me like I'm back as the kid again
I needed her spirit
brings me to life\

/good to see my old friend
my neighbor
good to tell him what I've been dealing with
to give me some advice quick
hand over the cover
of the males perspective\

/we made future plans
that would never come to life\

/you asked if we could meet in L.A.\

/rolling through the robey's
homies in the front seat
we're cruising around the city
it's golden hour
lounging in the car
I beg for more
he tells me to be patient
as he hands me a marijuana cigarette
that's a cheap vacation\

/lost time spent with you and I
staying up all night to lay in your arms
I'd take this as a pill
if I were ever lonely
wanna lay locked with you
in your arms just a little while
lounge with me in my honor

to drink this potion
as you follow the coastline, you can smell the ocean
calm is your hand as you run me through the motions

get lost in your day dreams
tranquility with the vibrations we lead
common is the seed
fill me up your basket
with lemon trees
take me with your empathy
sway me patiently
leave me in your arms would you please
love to lay with you next to me
don't sleep
we wanna ride out this day dream
summer wine
you and me kissing
lips so soft
don't wanna miss this
my mind replaying our love scenes
this ain't Christmas
coming back smelling up roses
with you here
smell of love in the air\

/there is no better moment than you telling me
that you cannot wait to see me again\

/we stayed up so late
talking and planning our trip to L.A.
both of us so excited\

/the love kills us
and then brings us back to life\

/loyalty before love\

/I thought I was doing the right thing
by keeping these secrets to myself
didn't wanna talk it off
just wanted it to vanish
like it never happened\

/I want to be draped in armor of your warmth energy
keep me wrapped up in your grasp
I want to be held
though I don't want to ask for it

I don't need you to shout out loud
I want you to feel this
I want to be loved for who I am
though I don't want to ask for it\

/I was going to see him soon
my stomach fluttered every time I thought of it\

/some days
I yearned for his affection
too much
like a child
whom wanted her mother just to smile at her
make it all feel better
like I'm losing focus without ya here
need you by my side
on this side we fight our demons here\

/slow responses
suddenly turned into no responses

I was left on read
that never happened\

/everything the light touches is in the palm of her hands
spun like wool
her hair to golden locks of fine jade jewels
whispered on the winds of curiosity
an iridescent personality
she sings of tunes that mimic her trauma
love bound, she finds solidarity in tranquility of the weeping wil-
    lows
which there hangs empty bottles
where she attempted to find herself
in the hollows, she still searches, in the depths of where she lies
    weak
motionless to speak
but not taken for the kill
water flowing heavily
heavy guilds the guilt
now there he goes, gasping for breathes that don't come easily to
    many men who stand up for raped women
they seem to drown with them
as I sink with them
we learn how to breathe under water
but everything the light touches is within her grasp\

/you still have people to meet
whom you'll fall in love with\

/splattered paint like the night sky
wrote patterns of you and I
they missed your light
called for you on set
last Friday night
miss no show\

/I could feel the distance
while he was telling me
there wasn't anything I was missing
everything was fine on his side
I was the one overthinking
he made me feel shitty for even mentioning it\

/I was exhausted of reminding him
to love me\

/don't gaslight me
when we both know the truth\

/am I a hypocrite for being mad at him for treating me how I
    treated him?\

/do not leave me to wonder
I'll trace it back years from now
I'll go back and forth
through our messages
play the investigator to see what happened
I'll rehearse our conservations back in my head
I cannot stop thinking of you\

/I'm sorry for the hurt I've caused you\

/I went on twitter
something I hadn't gone on in years

and looked at his tweets
there were sad subtweets about how he couldn't trust me
and how good he was to me
that he'd feed me grapes
bake me cakes
praising himself on his relationship skills
all around the time I cheated on him\

/it sounded like he was not too happy with me\
/I have to remind myself
that although the intention behind it might have been honest
the action still seeks the punishment\

the blame game–

/coke made me do it.

/communication flat lined
the time to go to L.A. was encroaching
my anxious heightened\

/sometimes
I'm better off with nobody\

/I am not a quitter
I may be a big fucking procrastinator
but I am not a quitter\

/living in stagnant conflict\

/I had half of a mind to think
he may not even show up to L.A.\

/radio silence from him
stuck like static to my ears
bleeding numb for his
numbed my hearing from all else
surrounded by ultraviolets
infused lighting

hit the ground running
no correct footing
keep missing you but you keep dodging my calls
do you not love me at all
baby where have you gone
loving you past dawn
won't wake you up
got a cup of coffee in the pot\

/when I finally reached him
it's a sword to my heavy chest
aches as I imagine giving birth
he acts completely unimpressed
speaking in a flat tone
as if it hadn't taken him 20 hours to text me back\

/I was shaking without him
the thought of being abandoned
I could not take it
I had a sick feeling he would leave me
stranded\

/I need lots of coffee and drugs to get through this\

/my head couldn't comprehend what must have happened\

/you never feel how much you love them
until you see them letting go\

/pushing me away
I'll push you farther back\

/come closer coward
tell me why you're hot n' cold\

/I could not let him see that I cared
I showed that side too much already
she's not coming out to play anymore\

/he claimed it was work that kept him from replying
but I know the tone of his voice
and it was chilling
and it was not the same voice\

/I knew in my heart
why it ached so much for his love
I knew it had left him
but it hadn't left me\

/L.A. was around the corner
and still I wasn't sure if he'd show up\

/sometimes I thought he wanted to pick a fight with me
just so he could call off meeting up in L.A.\

/you should never lose yourself in loving someone else
though I know this is easier said than done\

/the only thing you haven't broken yet
is that crystal fucking glass you sip out of\

/unlearning
self hate
is a tricky task\

/don't assume I was *only* the bad cop and he was the good cop in
      this scenario
remember most cops are bad\
/I don't know what made me more mad
his deafening silence
or the fact that he held so much power over me emotionally\

/all I wanted was him
I wanted us to be happy
I wanted to shower him in rainbows
I wanted to give him all of my love
I wanted to make him smile and to open his eyes and see me there
and him holding me
rocking me back and forth in your big arms\

/I was so desperate to see him
to make sure everything was okay
I wanted to fix this
whatever was going on\

/I would've paid the universe hundreds
just to have a one on one real heart to heart
conversation with him
the California man
I could feel he was exhausted of me
when I was begging for more of him\

/but I knew I wouldn't receive the answers I deserved to get
because he was a coward fronting like a gentleman\

/so he can post on his story
but not text me back?\

/I went to L.A.
I sat on that airplane
with a thousand paper cranes
dancing in my stomach
I knew this was not going to be easy
brace yourself,
I breathed out
as we took off\

/after the silence grew and grew
and the excuses piled on as to why he still hasn't shown up yet
I knew we were in for a shit show\

/what happened?
I cried out as I scrolled back through our text messages\

/I walked into the suite hotel room that we booked
I curled up in that big king bed
and cried while eating Doritos
wondering if he'd call soon\

/not knowing
is one of the worst feelings\

/just two weeks ago he was so excited to see me
now he goes ghost\

/damn
I didn't know Casper lived in California\

/did he have another girl?
did he find out about me and the coworker?
did he just not want to be with me anymore?
if that's the case than tell me
don't leave me to sit here sick to my stomach
wondering and wondering what happened
wondering if he'll show up ever\

/I'm not surprised anymore
I'm really not\

/waiting for your call
that never came\

/I flew from Chicago to California
to see my man
he was nowhere to be found
and I was the idiot who jumped on a plane to come all this way to
    see him
and he was the asshole who never showed up\

/yes he did
he left my ass in L.A.\

/and as those paper cranes flew away
I was left there
standing alone\

11. wounded woman

/I hope I don't bore you half to death
I mean, you did love me once\

/I wrote him,
if you cared about me

you'd tell me what happened,
I cried out
wanting to hear it spill from his fucking mouth
instead of someone else
if you cared you'd tell me,
...and all went dead
silent...
last text I'd ever write to him
while I stood there
sand in my toes
feeling as though I've won a thousand battles to come to the finals
to lose at the first round
karma comes back around
she doesn't miss her turn\

/telling me we would go back there
was just the lie you knew you needed to say in the moment\

/I am not ashamed for being a slut
I am not ashamed for being a slut\

/everything was so fine just two weeks ago...
oh boy, how things can change\

/I am in need of an emotional maid\

/I never cried so hard than I did in that hotel room\

/he left me there
stranded in L.A.
drowning in loneliness
I saw the devil in a white dress
while you smoke the devil's lettuce
I'll let you say less
keeping up with the usual suspects
could drop a dime faster for you to pick it up
rather than to call me back
your silence keeps your truth held
never cared to tell the truth did you?
leave me to answer it for us\

/to let someone come so close after this hurt?
how could you ask me to go near that once more
if possible to feel that pain

I will not feel that pain again
that is far too close
and I will not let them come close to me
I fear nothing more
than to feel this pain again\

/whoever said love is a drug
hit it on the motherfucking nail 'n coffin\

/each year
the swallows come back to Capistrano
and one came to me
singing,
I'll go back there someday
that I'd meet you again someday\

/the birds came to me
singing a different tune
while I whispered,

I'll take you to the other room
of beautiful things to come
share with me
one on one
as I woke up gasping
another day in L.A.
where you were not beside me\

/sorrow swallowed up my stomach
into criss cross knots
left me out to rout
sit and think of what I've done
learn what you have lost
there's no map to guide you
these steps are all on your own footing\

/I wanted the truth
I asked for it
but I feared the answer
sometimes the answer is worse than the question
though I reminded myself
to never be afraid of the truth\

/sometimes I need a fuckin shot of casamigos
and my best friends
'cause I can't do this shit alone\

/we pour that brown
just to drown
in it
that oblivion situation
needs no reservation
she just comes when she can
never mind the destination
nature state
I don't live in
city scape
he slides in
morning breaks
I see the escape
marked me late
two hours ago
sealed my fate\
/you lose him how you got him
and some things about a person never change
they just become more and more apparent until it's all that you can
    see\
/my head was in a fog about you
and why you left in such utter silence\

/be cautious of how many chips you decide to leave on the table
　　when you've never had a good hand
thing is, you're going to Vegas every time you gamble on a relation-
　　ship in your twenties\

/it's just messed up
how he gets to walk away
clean as a coward
and leave me to be the strong one
to travel and carry all of the hurt that he abandoned me with\

/I told myself
I wouldn't cry on another airplane\
/coming home
to collapse in sadness

/it was unfortunate
how I thought there was some sort of vengeance
in sleeping with someone else after he had left me
when I was left feeling more empty than before

and it reminded me
of why he left me in the first place\
/I came back to a cold climate
with a colder heart\

/it's quiet humiliating telling your parents
you got dumped on yet another vacation!\

/I wanted to hurt him
and make him feel it
burn
baby
burn
I want you to know how it feels
to suffer in silence\

/my stubbornness kicks boulders
even if they appear too heavy to move
as my fucking anxiety tap dances on my last damn nerves till the

next morning
nervous is my heart
to give up my heart to some other man that may not be as careful
    with it as I am
trust issues float to the top of the surface
meanwhile my soul ain't in service
come knocking on that intuition
is far too complicated to manipulate the decision
it's either your pride or your punishment
your commitment
choose whatever makes your more humbler in the moment
too brown eyed to see that green side of the fence
I see it in crimson colors as the fat lady dances\

/sometimes I'd rather take animal affection
than a man's affection\

/I think I love too much
I am afraid that the love others bring me won't ever be as fulfilling
as the love I could give to them\

/*he was probably too drugged out to remember,*
she told me\

/when they say
if you cant handle the heat get out of the kitchen
they weren't talking about the ovens or the flat tops
they're talking about the people\

/your silence
answered a lot of my questions\

/many times neglected
twice bitten
four times abandoned
never mentioned

she calls herself easy to manage
though she's high maintenance
when I'm high I maintain that shit

never basic
less I'm buying Starbucks
clout chaser
never mind Mr. President
he's too much of a hater

boolin' for the sake of it
doing donuts in the parking lot
just to talk to ya
final words
never mentioned
final words
God take me to heaven\

/morphed into an orbit of cluttered chaos
rummaging through lost thoughts
as I drink the venom my enemies poured up

resentment holds the burning torch
spiraled down
harder to pick you up with these press ons now
can't seem to forget the people who've betrayed me
feeling like the Count of Monte Cristo incognito
for the day
maybe
sing me to sleep, Frank Ocean
while I continue to drink this fucking potion\

/as I attempt to manipulate my mind
in forgetting him
I remember what it is I am trying to forget
while I begin to let him go
I continue to remember
my mind and body and soul
each one stained with a certain anguish facade
all of which I try to force my whole self
not to give into this suffocating pain\

/I wanted to forget him
but my love outweighed the hate
I could not find the words
our ending hadn't finished yet\

/I refused to let go
I held onto that rope
swinging my body back and forth
pleading for him to save me
come cut me down
and tell me why you left me here hanging\

/why do you continue to go back to him after he's done so many things to
    hurt you?
the girl with the violet eyes announced,
before I had a chance to come up with a good enough answer
she went on smoothly to say,
when the wolf attacks the fox, and the fox stays alive, she'd be a fool to go
    back to the wolf
and ask for him to lick her wounds\

/when a cynic falls in love
it can be catastrophic
releasing those indigo butterflies
with sativa smudged highs
it all comes in full
when we let go
and while I looked at these old photos of him and I
I knew neither of us would've thought how it'd end as it did
when things break between two cynics it's not just heartache
it's thunderstorms and hurricanes
we don't normally allow ourselves to fall victim to these emotions
so it's chaos when it finally rains\

/mom told me you can cure a wound with alcohol
the same way you cure a broken heart
with alcohol\

/ I remember a few years ago
I sold my soul to the devil
to make some chunks of change
the amount of money I made
wasn't worth how it chipped away at my mental state\

/creative people who take advantage of someone else's creative
    talents
to uplift their own art
that's some manipulative behavior\

/too many people are concerned about what you'll do for them\

/this world is built on collaboration
creative collection
create togetherness

Rome wasn't built by one person\

/it wasn't my fault other guys wanted to taste this too

/I deserve someone who comes to my front door
wanting to hear how my day was
I wanna ask,
when did you arrive?
and he replies,
every night
waiting for me to answer\

/you should have high standards
you're in control of who you surround yourself with
you're in charge of the energy that you create
you want to have high standards so that you only keep growing
we gotta keep moving
keep focused on who you want in your circle\

/just think of the man before him
you wouldn't have wanted anyone else but the man before him
but then you found him
and then next thing you know it's done
and again you can't imagine anyone else
or imagine yourself with anyone else
but like I said, you thought the same thing about the man before
    him
you'll find someone else again
and he'll leave and you'll think there's nobody else again
but there will be someone else after him too
there will always be somebody else\

/having what little hope I had
that everyday maybe he would call
I missed my California man so\

/I can't afford to care like this anymore
it's killing me
you are killing me
and I cannot allow myself to die along side you
I am not that girl\

/sitting out on that Logan Square roof top
to watch the harvest moon drop
smoking weed till the sun comes back up
selling lemon meringue
with not such sweet pain
she can't be alone
loving you will fade
likes to sip champagne
with his hand on her leg
partying in her past time
smoking weed to pass the time
time moves by so fast
she can't catch it
wasting away the days sleepin'
cause last night she missed it
she was at Liz's
partying with people she just met up with
what're you scared of?
of not making it?
while she falls down
the ladder
of climbing up to success
her day jobs are numbing her falls\

/I couldn't help but talk about him
and I eventually bored myself

with talking to myself about him\

/it's like standing in a hot kitchen all day
sweating out the sadness and the liquor from your pores
of past night sores
feels good to be angry sometimes\

/feels worse
to be hungover when you're heartbroken\

/you flaunted like you're some perfect human
that you were this kid who was gonna to be greater than his father
that's what I admired
your aspiration
your determination
but after it was all sudden done
you want so many things
but you never worked for them
you never truly worked at anything you wanted beyond what you
    already had

you stayed comfortable in the idea of obtaining
waiting for these opportunities to present themselves
rather than being a fighter on the front lines
nothing just comes to us because we will it
you could've done more
you could've been more
but you aren't a Michael
you're a Fredo to me at this point\

/the route of all anger is sadness
there is no kind of rage without deep suppressed sorrow
look at anything you've ever had anger towards and tell me that
    that wasn't sadness at the end of the day
letting yourself feel hurt instead of pretending that it's only hate
    which drives you
is accomplishing one act of growing up
and the other act of letting go
these are the stages of becoming a mature adult\

12. a healing woman

/I've learned
in order to evolve
you need to eliminate\

/sometimes, I imagine myself dying
just to envision what kind of reaction I would get out of him
isn't that so fucked up? To go so far as to contemplate my own
    death, because that would *clearly* be the only way to get a
    reaction out of a person who's supposed to love me while I am
    breathing\

/when the pain hit
it melted to my brain
like slow sweet honey
sugar cane
dripping from your lips
all the way to my finger tips
back to my lips
one last time
reminding me of how good this love tastes
that I won't be able to try the flavor of you again
it was nice knowing you
old friend\

/don't go near the pictures
the videos
or the 35mm film photos taped onto the corner of your bedroom

wall
of where he looks sexy
and where he looks at you like he's infatuated
and where you look euphorically happy
try not to look at those... they'll break your heart all over again\

/I knew he must've been hurting
too
and what killed me
is I wanted to lay beside him
to help heal his pain\

/it was as if you had no remorse
in losing me
losing me did not matter to you
how could you be so callous
walking around bare footed in Paris
hooded eyebrows
can't see clearly beyond the surface
with xanned out lens
this view is muted\

/I don't know what it is about me

though I've tried my whole life to decipher
if caring too much about others
is a character flaw,
or am I just so soaked in stubborn loyalty
that I am incapable of brutal betrayal like so many of my peers
    seem to feel no compassion for
even so, I get frustrated with myself
how I have found too many times laying in bed alone
feeling this immense amount of sadness and grief for those I've
    loved who have hurt me
I find myself consumed in this weird sympathy which I try to
    submit
I wish I could find vengeance in their sadness
I can't find that
not for the one's who I've loved
and maybe that is love
maybe that's maturing
maybe that's just me
that no matter what, if I love you, I'll always have love for you
and I can't help in wanting to be the one to save you from your own
    self harm
from your own self hate
wish I could help you
I wished you would've let me help you
I wish I could've been the person to kill your demons along side
    you
and even though you're the reason I am hurting, I know you're
    hurting more
I know you're more than this

more than the villain
more than an anti-hero
more than the drugs that consume you
to forget all this
I saw so much in you
so much greatness
and I am scared
I do not take joy in your suffering
you're more than how it ended
with heartbreak from your own hurricane
or maybe you're the one tapping me awake
begging me to forgive you for your sadness
for your mistakes
though it will never be the same and that in itself is hard to over-
    come
to admit how I love you after what you had done
you asked if we could go back there
we'll go back to that motel someday, you whispered
and all I could think
in reminding myself
of how ironically life comes full circle
yet again
I was so heavily heartbroken in a desert
only two years ago
by the musician
and somehow
I fell so in love with my California man
in the desert
as long as I could I wanted that motel

I wanted that desert
we should have stayed there, I thought over the phone with him
that seemed to be the only time where the both of us had com-
      pletely forgotten how the rest of the world existed, I forgot that
      there was more to the world than just the two of us
consumed in an utter love trance
mesmerized by the addictive feeling
the two of us had never experienced
wanting to feel this way
always
I wanted to feel this again
and I knew he wanted to feel this
more than I did
I wish we could go back there... I said so quiet only God could hear
while my whole body ached
in dreaming to go back
desperate in longing to relive that moment
over and over
or once more
to feel real true love
we'll go back there, he sounded so sure of himself
giving me his word, but it was to me
only a whisper in the wind
half way across the country
that would hopefully wander its way back to us
...though, that is what I wanted to believe, and he was too ignorant
      to see the truth...
I promise, we will go back there, he said convinced over the phone
though, I didn't have the heart to say, like he did not have the heart

to believe
that we would never go back there\

/my feelings are valid and I shouldn't have to explain it to anyone
I am exhausted of people telling me I shouldn't care about him
    anymore
I loved him, and I still care
if I did not care now, then I myself would argue was that ever love
    to begin with?
but do you assume I want to feel this way?
do you think me being a woman, that I really want to continue
    after this is over, to continue to still feel remorse for his own
    sadness?
I fucking hate that I hurt to know that he hurts
that I bleed when I feel him bleeding
but i do still love him
and that's what is really driving me crazy
but I can't help it
I feel it
I am trying to ignore it but still it is there
it lives in me
for now
so don't look at me like I am crazy
cause I feel crazy enough that I still have love for him\

/people who talk shit
don't have shit to talk about\

/I don't have time to worry about you
I am too busy getting this money
and making my art\

/I realized
I needed Rihanna energy for this break up\

/I'm on some
I'll come at your whole motherfuckin' life in a matter of three min-
    utes or less 'cause you ain't got much of a life outside me\

/his worst fear was answering to me
my worst fear was him never answering\

/when I am at a loss, art will always find what I cannot speak out
  loud\

/I feel as though I am morning a loss of a person who is still alive,
  but feels dead in my heart\

/switching from cannabis to CBD oil
is like switching from coffee to tea
I just can't do it\

/we all come in waves of ourselves\

/I've lived another year in this simulation
and I feel like I am getting the hang of this shit
but that's what I thought a year ago\

/I've realized I love too much
and that I have never been properly appreciated for what I do give
only longer than temporary lust which was masked as love
I've never had somebody love me equally
or the way that I wanted to be loved
I have always catered to them,
I have always given them the love they wanted
to the best of my abilities\

/in a game of tug of war
I found that grief is a place where your unexpressed love is stored

I tire myself out yet again
filling my baggage to the brim

I find that I can't hide my tracks if I don't lift my weight
I see that weakness is never praised

and ask myself
why am I so exhausted

to find somebody who'll respect my body
should not be so difficult
but they seem to find me where I'm most vulnerable

how low I found myself when I really think of it
feeling as though I am chained down

that it takes all of me to move
maneuvering through life in a lukewarm swimming pool\

/I have learned to love myself when there wasn't a single human
      around
we are selfish creatures
each of us
yearning for affection and greed and power
we need to learn balance
simplicity is key
nature does not over take her fill
she is generous with her wealth
we take and take
and then we ask why we aren't full
we need to make of what we have
and gave to others who do not have the privilege like we do
giving to others will fill you too\

/get into good routines
smarter habits
sleep more
our mental state depends immensely on our sleep

drink water
take care of yourself\

/sometimes you need to just release all of that pent up emotion
scream about it to yourself
write it down
punch a pillow
than reconsider letting it finally go\

/ways to increase your endorphins naturally
eating chocolate and chili peppers
going outside in the sun
drinking red wine
having sex
or masturbating
laughing
exercising
aromatherapy
animals\

/how come a man is a man
based on how much p*ssy he gets?
but a woman is a slut based on how much d*ck she gets?\

/thank you,
to my guy friends
whom instilled wisdom on the logic of a males perspective and
    feelings
and let me in on their secrets
that men are emotionally unintelligent
and non confrontational\

/don't just learn from your mistakes
make actions to change\

/if you want something
you need to work your ass off for it
everything in life is a work in progress
life changing experiences are never met
without elimination

and growth
and knowledge\

/*stop feeling fucking sorry for yourself,*
I told myself\

/I was in that phase where I had to post on Snapchat just to re-
    mind the California man
that I was thriving without him
that I am sexy and beautiful
and every time he watched my story
it gave me some sort of validation
like he cared about me
or some shit?
when all he's really doing is tapping one time on a screen and
    watching a ten second video of me?
you don't matter that much\

/it was very difficult having my best friend be so extremely close to
    him
because in my heart
I never wanted to hear of him again

every time he crossed my mind
sadness bloomed inside\

/my best friend was especially caring about us breaking up
she treated my wound
nursing me back to health
I loved her more than him
she was my best friend
my first girl friend in Chi town
and she stuck to me like peanut butter and jelly
blood orange serenaded her aura
she was a character like no other
her and the California man
grew up together as children
I would never want to break their bond
I loved the two of them as friends
seeing their dynamic
was electric
they loved each other
but I knew apart of it had diminished
because of how everything had finished\

/but I will never forgive him
for what he did to you... it's unforgivable,
she said to me\

/make a mountain in your mind
prove that it can not only be shaken but it can be moved\
/revaluate your current situation
who are the five people you're most close to?
who is your support system?
who loves you the most?
who do you admire?
you are the sum of your five closest friends
you are the energy you surround yourself with
you should have support other than yourself
you should have somebody who loves you immensely
you should have one person you look up to
revaluate your current state\

/the violence against women in the media is excruciatingly painful
to see

women having to match up to these outrageous standards just to
feel beautiful

having to fit in this hourglass mold of a woman

what makes us different is what makes us beautiful
the way women our age compare themselves to other women
it is always a negative outcome of women shaming other women
    for their body image
we are made the way we are for a reason
our bodies are our homes
they are our gardens

I've had a lot of turmoil with body dysmorphia
seeing myself as too thin
that my ass isn't as big as it used to be
or my stomach is now too big but nothing else has grown in the
    right places
or I have too much hair
that my face isn't thin enough

I've neglected to feed my body the love that it deserves
I found that I should never let the competing comparison of any
    other woman stand in the way of seeing my body as beautiful\

/I'm convinced
life is preprogrammed\

/shout out to my guy friends
the one's who've protected me
thank you
and especially to the one's who're feminists
thank you\

/took a trip to florida
just to see the local boy club\

/I love the ocean beneath my feet
and the waves coming to console my body
relinquish my past experiences\

/you aren't going against the "bros"
when you agree with a woman over another man's opinion\

BLOOD ORANGE

/to be quite honest,
I think we're all a little bi-curious
at some points\

/I will always be a free spirit
it hurts to be alone
but the wind keeps calling me\

/he holds me close
although I am closed
he assumes I am open because of the way that I touch him
the systematic of my voice how it swirls
like drizzled caramel and chocolate milk

he's used to getting with many girls but this girl he cannot figure
    out
as I clutch the sand in my stubborn fist
to get away from my anger towards another man whom is not him
I feel so trapped in my own olive skin
I am suddenly consumed with violets
from my toes
to my chest

to the ends of my curls
though, don't be mistaken, I do not bloom like these other heart-
    broken girls

to that night on the beach,
whispers of how he cannot stop fantasizing about Carmen
I tell him,
keep dreaming,
he mutters,
don't sleep on me,

I understand how you don't have trust in these men,
as he twists his fingers around my head
to kiss my hair
lay my curls on his chest
while I look away from him
staring at the sea
the waves mimic like steel swords slashing down to the shore
recognizing ahead of time that I am already five feet back
from where he stands
though he cannot recognize this
because *he is not him*
and he is not him
I've become a professional
at giving the grand illusion of false affection
I wear a mask others cannot find in my dirty closet
fabricated love that I was meant to give to somebody else instead
but I pretend
and he ends up hurt in the end

but he is not him
and he is not him

my mind races to find a duplicate
to fill where he no longer lives

so desperate for his love again
I try to give my energy to any other man deemed fit who lay beside
    me
to move on
to forget
and in my mind, I want somebody to love me just as he did

fill my tank with nicotine let me breathe out these toxic dreams
so I'll spend the night with you
giving out the affection I was saving for him
and as I sit here with my coffee filled to the brim
with mediocre fake love and a joint in my hand
to get me through these lies that I've lived
questioning how two people can love each other but not make it fit
as I listened to the conversation growing rapid
and his affection for me is heightened
I don't want him to hurt, but my broken heart selfishly loves the
    attention
and I know I am a bastard
for constantly looking to see some characteristics of him in them
but silence arises and now all I see is the ocean rising
It grows deafening
as I shrink slower

the cynic in me comes closer
and the color of violet bleeds darker
and darker
but he is not him
and I say to myself,
he is not him

and I feel a fool to play the part of missing a man who no longer
    wants my love in his grasp
and listening to this nice guy desire me, while I can't take the
    chance
because he is not him
and he is not him

as I stare at the ocean
wishing this man next to me
would completely vanish
and I'd stand here alone
listening to these gruesome tides explode
to accept the fact that you can't find him in somebody else
and he can't find you in anybody else

I am trying to learn how to see him separate
from all men

but nobody else is him
and nobody else will love me like him

/he coughed out sweet loving lines
I said,
don't get me sick,
I can't catch what you have

/when you know it's not going to work out
but you're just desperate for love and affection\

/I think losing is worse than winning\

/I will not be anyone's consolation prize\

/I am what others are afraid to be
I don't know why I'm attracted to men who can't love me
that's a fuckin' bad habit
I wish I weren't a nicotine addict
I wish I smoked marijuana less
I wish my relatives respected my so called success
I wish these panic attacks weren't so frightening

I wish I hadn't put my parents through some type of hell
I wish my anxiety wasn't a bitch
I wish social media wasn't at the forefront of our generations
    minds\

/the divine
feminine
ooh how she shines
like diamonds
elevate your subconsciousness

go towards a place you want to live in

relinquish all your past ingredients
come to me for the recipe
I have the experience
tranquility breeds the innocent

the survived Phoenix
glides through the matrix
like the Lebanese dancers remix
trying to find a square to fit into a wooden peg
to fit inside your mind
the divine
feminine
ooh how she has melanin

dipped in her skin
doesn't vanish in her lingerie fashion
trying to climb up that ladder
to success
her sex life
is numbing her falls\

/the girl with the violet eyes asked me what I believed in
and I am realizing as I grow older
that faith is becoming harder and harder to hold onto\

/I ain't no hussy man,
I ain't no motherfuckin hussy,
but everybody loves
Lucius and Cookie

I bulldoze through men n call that a big production
make my baby some steak and potatoes
call that a home supper
she scored LeGrant from the minor leagues
call that a home runner
she works a 9-5 at the club

with the big, red bottoms on
call that a big stunner\

/there are a fewer things more satisfying than seeing your ex three
    months later
looking like the damn front cover of another D.A.R.E's ad,
may, *"welcome to Applebee's, can I take your god damn order?"* Be a
    sweet melody stuck in his xanned out head
and I'm over here feeling and looking fye as hell
and he's getting some goth crackhead from his high school sliding
    into his dms
and I got a dude from the minor leagues hitting me up
whadda ya got?
a Rebecca looking ass... nice
is that a full on titty profile picture?
a real class act ya got there\

/finally,
my best friend confessed to me about why he left
she admitted to telling him about me and the coworker
a few weeks before LA
and that he told her he decided to leave me because I slept with my
    co worker and lied

apparently he said that he couldn't take the fact that we were in an
    open relationship
he hated that I was sleeping with other people\

/*he was begging me to tell him who you'd slept with*
apparently he knew you were lying,
she admitted to me that night\

/*I couldn't lie to him,*
she murmured\

/I forgave her for telling him,
because I should've been the one to tell him
before she had\

/girlfriends come before him\

/I wished he had just confronted me about this
I wished I had told him the truth
before our mutual best friend did\

/it is a curse and a blessing
sharing a best friend with your ex\

/it's hard to be sober
when you're this depressed\

/so you're gonna leave me 'cause I get around a little bit
and yet you have some stripper all up on your twitter?
c'mon now\

/*I am a woman*
I do not put other women down
I will help build other women up

I have to remind myself of this
because I can be petty too\

/I like being in the mad
fuck you
stage of a break up
I need some damn comedy in my life
c'mon
this shit is overwhelming depressing\
/I suppose
I am the broken, underdog too
they just rarely have a female in these roles
so it must've slipped my mind\

/I wondered if he went through the motions
of missing me too\

/I cannot stress this enough
if someone isn't willing to sacrifice one honey bee
when you've given them their second hive?
reevaluate\

/found my third eye,
at the bottom of my first cup of black coffee\
/took a tab
woke up in a new dimension\

/I slink my body back to you
again
growing thorns each time I sin
cut me deep
limb from limb
she runs the cold blade across my finger tips
cool chef knife tricks
captured in one night
by a flight of parachute lights
lonely lives the life
night breaks and she knows she shouldn't have seen him again
kissed her fate\

/choke me stiff into a corset

then they give me permission to breathe

Criss-crossing
in penciled in thin linings
of the line women have to walk down finely
to adapt into todays society
is not a tightrope men would wish to walk across
it's just a cross we bare
come now,
sit in our chair
and turn the mirror

what men don't understand
what they lack is knowledge of their other halves
what they lack is what does not directly affect them
but you don't have to take my word for it
I'll just word vomit all over your daddy's closet

I took too much for my plate
intending to feed other woman
though I am not accomplishing what I think I am making

I've never had good patience
clumsy when I'm anxious
feeling anxiously slept on from a man who I just slept with
there's nothing new about that

continued onto my past
doused in misogynistic men

letting their words about my body
fluttered in and out of my pretty little head\

/my favorite sex position
being the god damn CEO of these mofos\

13. natural born woman in the wild

midnight in the garden of good and evil–

/he comes to me at night
although I am dreaming
and I wonder if this is where we meet again
for the reality of us is no longer breathing
so we find each other in the crypts of a dangerous Neverland

swirling around in love that we imagined never grew dead
down and down we spin
though I wake up
and he is miles away from where I lay my head\

/I fell asleep loathing the idea of love
and I wake up missing the thought of being loved\

/I needed a palette cleanser
from men\

/you can tell a lot about a person
by how they came into your life
and how they left it looking\

/the key is to find something tangible
something that makes us happy

stop using men as a guilty hobby
we're stronger than that\
/I find it very amusing
the amount of men I've heard slut shamming women who sleep
    around
yet in the same breath they expect us to be as experienced as their
    favorite porn stars?
c'mon now\

/I don't take money from men
making my own money
makes me happy\

/I was meant to drive a Mercedes Benz\

/if you can focus on manifesting wealth
it will come to you in multitudes of fashions\

/having true friends in life is one of the greatest gifts
God can offer\

/go towards what calls your spirit the loudest\

/karma is real
cash in on her good side\

/recognize the bad traits you have
be self diligent
notice your triggers
the word is overused but it is significant to your mental health
when you get overwhelmed with depression or anxiety
remind yourself to do opposite to emotion
when I feel anxious
I tend to over think
I breathe heavier
I talk too much about every possibility in my head
I've found now that when I notice myself getting into that
I practice my breathing

I write about the situation on paper in three different versions
most of the time I'll work on my art and use music therapy
or take a walk
getting yourself out of that zone is key to gaining better copping
    skills\

/most people would say,
to the strong women out there
or,
to the beautiful women out there
but I leave it simply to,
all of the women out there
who are we to decide what is strength
and what is beauty
each person sees beauty or strength in different obstacles
in different shades of skin color
in different body types
though I beg of the world to see more beauty in woman and in
    men
by the size of their characters
by their intentions
for their aspirations
for their attitudes when situations get rough
why do we measure beauty by body type
there is so much more to us
many people chose to be lazy

they look at the cover
instead of reading the back of the book\

/when humans focus a lot of energy solely on themselves
they lose sight of the world around them
try being an observer for once
it could change the way you see yourself too\

/bury me
in Coco Chanel
a spliff between my nimble fingers
and don't forget my Tabasco sauce\

/it baffles me
the amount of times
when I first meet a man
how my kindness is often taken for,
oh, she wants to have sex
and when they take that
and run with it

BLOOD ORANGE

I immediately become standoffish
which to them almost always seems to translate to,
oh, well she's just a tease then\

/don't be deceived
a woman with a man can be hurting alone
possibly even more so, than a single woman
I have felt both situations
and both times I ask myself the same question
why do I feel so alone?\

/you can't expect someone else to change for you\

/listen to your god damn instincts like it's God whispering in your
    damn ear\

/I get high
and he becomes him\

/I remember how we used one and other
two friends
two neighbors
drowning in two different sullen heartbreaks
baby, lay with me,
let's make this pain go away,
he looks at me in that red dress
and I looked at him
with his curly, dark hair
dripping like chocolate cherries
hadn't looked at him like that in ages
we were both desperate for any connection
pretending like we loved each other for the time being
using one and other but not admitting it
and after it was all set and done
I looked at my friend
and said,
once more?... for old time's sake?\

/I woke up there
next to him
I remembered how I dreamt of this day
waking up next to him
and not feeling guilty
years later
and now I wish there was no man here

to lay beside me
I wanted to be alone\

/I wasn't worried about the neighbor and I
things would always be like this between us
and I suppose
I wouldn't have it any other way
and yet it was a very different feeling
not the same kind I felt all those years ago\

/I sat in my Wicker Park windowsill
just as the sun rose
to listen to the birds chime and hum
I sparked up an old blunt
and looked back at the man sleeping soundly in my bed
curled up
I sighed
wishing my neighbor would walk home soon\

/all I wanted
was to be alone
in silence
no men on my mind
I've decided
they can hide in my blind spots
I don't see y'all\

/yet
in the back of my mind
I was still waiting for him to call\

/my mom used to say to us:
go towards the path that your spirit cries out loudest for
I know now
what she means\

/cooking food
and binge eating
while watching bad TV
is my go to ex\

/I don't go back to my ex's after we're done
I go back to these bad television reruns\

/I don't know why this shocks me so much
when people go back to their ex's
I could never go back to my ex's
they've done extremely fucked up things to end the relationship
I would look like a desperate woman taking them back

you don't eat fast food leftovers
unless you're significantly desperate\

/feeling anger creates more adrenaline than sadness
I wear my emotions like a sleepless Sunday hang over
before work in an hour
8 hour shift and no money for a 14 dollar Lyft
it's surge prices

political warfare devices

hidden behind those badges you wear so proudly
behind that weapon you use to announce me
these police in these streets

they gunned those boys down
sounds of fireworks shot 10 rounds
desensitized to violence now

these conversations are political
yet it's basic human rights we're speaking about
it's not unusual
you just decided to attend the daily funeral

nobody's forcing you to listen
we
speak the same languages
yet we lack so much communication\

/when I take sexy pictures of myself and post it
that's for me
nobody else
it's not to show off or to prove anything
I do it because it makes me feel good
and my beauty can be shown publicly
without it being a monopoly
and if you don't relate to this
than you love yourself less\

/I manage the jumbled up emotions
falling through open skylight windows
I mourn the loss of a thousand fallen warriors
who've laid down their swords in my honor
they cannot fight my war
as the body keeps score
flesh and blood
wounded woman run amuck
of times lost and times never forgotten
she falls deeper into depression
to them, the ones who've stolen her body
who've claimed her temple as their pit stop

she asks me how i am feeling
of those nights
how they left a sour taste
no food in my belly
the mood doesn't change
and yet I filled their plates
they have no idea
the mistakes they've made
the trauma they've inflicted upon me
bones bruised on my miniature, stolen body
you held me down while I was fighting
buried me three feet underneath
no breathing techniques to cope with this type of heat
trauma doesn't sleep
as the body keeps score

boom, boom,
bang, bang
there goes my heart and shame
weaving through life like strobe lights
slowly
it takes a lot to know nobody
fleeting fast my beating chest
can't sleep cause I'm stressed

saw my twin flame
in my dreams
he whispers subtly
wondering where my invisible wounds are stored

as the body continues to keep score
...as the body continues to keep score...\

/determination is key to success
don't feel overwhelmed because you don't have it all just yet\

/no one knows you like your mother knows you\

/there is birth control for men
so why are we shooting bullets at a bullet proof vest?
instead of taking the bullets out of the barrel\

/I agreed to go out with him
he took me to a comedy show that wasn't that funny
but the bad script made us laugh
we shared drinks over polite conversations
the mood felt different
like a weird, new beginning
ever since we had sex things changed
my neighbor was a new man\

/we didn't have sex that night
we didn't kiss either
and apart of me was relieved
and the other half wanted to see him try
just to know if he wanted to or not
maybe it was just a one time thing\

/I can't stand b*tchy co workers
we all have to be here?

why do you have to be so negative?\

/it's hard being an entrepreneur
while also working for *"the man"*
people love to take advantage of your talents
for small wages\

/I always try to remind myself to rise above
the pettiness
though it can be difficult sometimes
at the end of the day
you can look back and say that *you didn't* put negative energy out
    there
they did\

/I've had some serious fucking beef with some serious douche-bag
    cooks\

/after awhile

I couldn't take the misogyny in the kitchen
it was dripping in sweaty male ego
festering with underlining racism and prejudices
sitting in a sauna full of thirsty men
the kitchen breeds assholes or strong chefs
there can only be two
I promise you
there are only two types
of chefs or cooks
in the kitchen\

/they taught me how to fight for myself
they taught me how to use my voice
and how to make it sound louder
they taught me how to believe in God
when so much of my faith was crumbling
they taught me how to work for what I want
when I felt as though I had nothing\

/after the misogyny
lack of respect
screaming on the line
the fights
the discord
cheap ass wages

the amount of labor
management was inconsistent
I had to quit
once I did
the crew followed suit with quitting too\

/my now old boss
with the one bedroom apartment in the sky
and the gold chains
I caught him shaking in his shinned boots
when the crew quit
he didn't know the voice I had in that kitchen
he underestimated me
and the impact I made to that family\

/I wasn't expecting them to quit when I did
though they deserved better
as I did\

19. bohemian woman becomes a luxury brand

/connections
networking
friendliness
communication
breeds opportunities
remember this in life
you don't know who'll be your next connection\

/difficult to take a woman from the ghetto
make her wear stilettos\

/if I hadn't made that connection with Diego a year ago
and then ran into him at Target three weeks ago...
for him to recommend me
I wouldn't have gotten this job\

/before I quit
I secured a job to hit
with a big hotel in downtown Chicago
off of Michigan avenue
on the roof top
making 25 an hour
I was gaining that good karma\

/I wanted to take all of my hard working coworkers with me
primarily the beautiful women in the kitchen
they were my family
aside from the misogynistic men

women are the ones who hold the kitchen together
while the men keep it in utter discord
women have to work ten times harder to prove themselves
especially in the kitchen
the standard women have to uphold in comparison to what men
    have to prove...\

/I have to admit
it was addicting having somebody miss you
and long for you
when it's so accessible
its not as valuable\

/I wished I could've
taken them with me
they deserved the money
they deserved the luxury of this new job
it would've changed their lives
going from 13 an hour to 25
and something inside of me felt so sad
that I couldn't carry them on my back
to lead them to this other small victory\

/saying this goodbye was very difficult
yet rewarding in some ways
working for this ship for three years of my life
I discovered things I wouldn't have learned anywhere else
I discovered people I wouldn't have met anywhere else
and I thank the coworkers
the ones who were my family
thank you
for bathing me in rainbows
when my color had been drained
thank you for carrying me on your tired backs when I had no
    strength to move
thank you for showing me what hard work and determination
    really means\

/black women are the most under appreciated and under accepted
    women
in our country
black women are the most unloved women in our country
black women are the most misrepresented women in our country
why when the media portrays black women in a positive light it's
    almost too often met with just *"strength" or "bravery"*
which are very accurate qualities
but why aren't black women portrayed as beautiful?
why not beautiful?
black women are the most beautiful women in our country\

/I stepped into my new environment
blooming with vigorous talent
felt like I was competing on *Top Chef*
every day I walked into that kitchen
combined with fresh seafood
waygu steak on the grill
an herb garden in the basement
on top of a very tall building
overlooking the downtown chi city\

/the older generation is so damn judgmental
I'm not coming at religion here
but doesn't it say in the Bible to love thy neighbor?
it never said to judge a person for loving someone of the same sex\

The pauper becomes the princess-

/I felt like I was a girl taken from the ghetto
and dropped into the lux of Chicago\

/it is a whole different mood
working off of Michigan avenue
where the luxury brands linger
and the prices go up
went from artificial flowers
to petals of roses and dangling diamonds
from florescent lights
to chandelier lighting\

/try your best to be aware of cultural appropriation\

/you lingered on my mind
a little bit too much\

/I hate seeing my abusers being praised
I hate seeing my friends abusers being praised
I hate seeing abusers being praised\

BLOOD ORANGE

/we as women
should uplift one and other
we should not be jealous of our sister's
we should be determined to help each other succeed
it is our time to fight back
thank your mom
thank your grandma
for making this path for our generation as women
thank them for making this walk easier on our feet\

/my mom would tell me
how lucky I was to have grown up in this generation
you have no idea
how hard it was for women\

/real generous people are the best kinds of people\

/I cannot bleed this dark shade of violet anymore
for men who've hurt me
I cannot put energy into why they've damaged me
I cannot put energy into my broken heart
I need to be stronger for myself
I need to be better than this
and use my hurt to fuel my art
each day that passes that I lack improvement
can only injure my own future
nobody else's
think of how foolish that is
to drown for a man who wouldn't care to see me swim\

/striving alone
is my favorite flex\

/airdrop him a nude one of these days\

/don't need no men's money
I make my own\

/once I got my paycheck
I went to Adidas
to buy that matching track suite
all yellow baby
sleek and comfy
don't ever say I rained on your parade
cause I am a ray of sunshine
on your darkest day\

/once you've become aware of feeling blessed for what you do have
and begin to make plans to achieve what you don't have
life will not feel so heavy this time around\

/I've noticed
after dabbling with some horrible people
I've become a better person\

/y'all men
will be too horny
and miss out on a real home girl\
/every single person on this earth has value
and it is not measured by how you look\

/I missed the girl with the violet eyes
she played puppeteer to the cosmos
and I wondered why they let her pull the strings\

/I could careless of what a man thinks of me
in relation to my looks
I will not trim
or shave my body to his liking
this is my home
I have to live in it
I will not change the color of this room to match his preference\

/hmm who be that
crumbled in my mouth like Scooby snacks
bad head giving ass
he can't last longer than 3 minutes
came back around just to call me fat
insecure ass
hmm who be that?
oouu you said my ass is a little flat?
so you got the audacity to give me that back?
bitch,
you never licked this
you deserve a pancake ass
to go with your breakfast sausage sized dick\

/time
is
money
and you aren't paying me to waste my time\
/I've dealt with a lot of petty men\

/the media makes women out to be crazy
but why don't they turn the camera towards these psychotic men
in my opinion
men are more crazy
they make us out to be insecure
men are more insecure than women are
they just have a different way of showing it
they just have a different way of hiding it\

/our generation claims to be so welcoming
and yet we're the most insecure
most judgmental generation about outward appearance
everyone is so picky about our looks now a days
does personality even matter anymore?\

/am I the only one that gets turned on by a great personality
rather than a hot body?
I don't care about what you look like
if you can make me laugh
babe you're half way there\

/I like men that are less attractive than me
because he can know wholeheartedly
that he has a bad bitch\

/all I am going to say is
let these motherfuckin' men know
let them know who they have\

/when I went to the hospital
the receptionist saw I was going through it
I was getting checked for a possible STD
she looked me dead in the eyes and said sternly,
always protect yourself
always look out for your body
these men will not
I am fifty years old and they're still on these games
listen to me
always protect yourself\

/you think it won't catch up to you
but it will\

/I foolishly assumed it would never happen to me
don't count yourself out\

/these things are very common
yet we are ashamed to address them, because of the stigma attached
but because we neglect to talk about these sexual diseases
it continues more frequently
because it is not on our forefront to get checked
it is so important to go and get checked
take care of yourself
do what you need to do
to protect yourself
your body deserves to be taken care of\

/men give me a migraine\

/smoking sativa
just to get high with ya
I'm going to numb my pain
for the time being
hearing that shame
hiding away his name

she plays so beautifully
the saxophone in the rain
while I dream
the girl with the violet eyes carries me through the seams
created from translucent memories
of things that may not be
of racing
of running too fast
of dodging every bad comment ever had
anxiety ridden
chaos driven
let the sax play slowly
drum beat baby
my spaghetti lady
beating my neighbor home
gonna make him some homemade dinner\

/seeing my drag queen best friend
in her glamour state

seems to melt my pain
hiding away like Batman
where's my Robin
seems times been robbing me blind of my sins
working 24 hours just to make rent\

/seeing him
helped me heal\

/that night
he told me over red wine,
I'll always have something for you,
I rocked back in my chair
and said,
oh, really\

/I've found I have to love certain people
even for opposing opinions

people will not always understand or agree with how the world
    should work
it doesn't always mean they're a bad person
they see the world differently\

/it baffles me
the misconception
of letting go
people want to hold on too much
they want to pour all their energy in enabling them to carry around
    a toxic, heavy relationship
because they assume they'll be so much weaker without it
but how can you be strong if you continue to hold onto a relation-
    ship that is paining you to carry?
you never know your strength till you let go
you will notice
how your arms can now carry
what you could not have bared before\

/what's worth it to you?
what gives you life?\

/success turns me on\

/go looking for people
where you'd want to find them\

/I was in a relationship
where he wanted me there always
but wasn't willing to put in *enough* effort to make me feel like he
    wanted me there
the last and the first man I ever loved left me stranded in LA
yet, I've never owned up to the fact that I loved him
I am ashamed for a lot of the guys I chose to have sex with out of
    self sabotaged behavioral problems I've seemed to call I de-
    served
I've lost a lot of passion due to my exhausted anxiety
trauma never tires
in turn I need to be stronger
I find it very difficult to ask for help, because I want to be the
    healer,
not the one needing the healing
I have philophobia
I hate that I care too much,
that my empathic ways effect so much of my soul

I am tired of defending women to men who don't seem to have
    women to educate them
I am sick of holding it down for men who don't appreciate my
    strength
I still hold on too tightly to this rage of how things ended with him
I continue to harbor anger on my past friends
who've stabbed me in the back
even from years ago
and I want to trust him but I can't
but none of these men ever seem to be different
even the uglier ones still manage to fuck you over\

/say it again,
I am a fine ass
dope ass person
and I deserve better\

/I tried to be a new woman
to tidy up the apartment
float along in my pink lingerie
throw roses over my balcony
see the sky for what it is
bask in the moment

release some of that pent up echoing ego
become one with myself
in tune with Mother Earth
she is our guild to a better world
being at first glance
focusing on smoking less
possibly give this guy a second chance\

/the girl with the violet eyes called me one day
she was coming home from Paris\

/sneaking out to smoke some weed
childish fiend
I am about that green
money making machine
she manifests destiny
capitalism is a fucking monopoly
pyramid scheme
don't sign me up for the team
call me cleopatra cause I'm climbing up that ladder
way higher
slow dancer
make that Lebanese shake her-

ask later\

/read both sides of the argument\

/I gave so much of me to you
and then you left me as if I were nothing
I could never do that to someone
and that's the terror in it all
of giving too much of your self to someone
for them to leave
as they steal apart of you
that you thought was shared\

/the neighbor understood
knowing what I was going through
he sympathized with my pain
and he knew how to set me on fire
his spirit echoed mine\

/nostalgias cold knife ran a blade across my eye
ice cool
yet felt like fire
I missed this liar
I missed my desire
I missed seeing her inspired
I missed the girl with the violet eyes
like a loyal dog to her owner
I missed her\

/there was nothing more desirable
than summertime
in Chicago\

/one night
drunk on summer wine
over looking the city
sitting on that old echoing light house
not the same one as we did as kids
this one was farther north
we looked out at the dazzling city
hearing the echoes of what the aphrodisiac potions created
as he looked at me

I saw him as a young kid again
only 19
while in a daze
he leaned in and kissed me
I closed my eyes
and I remember feeling my heart drop\

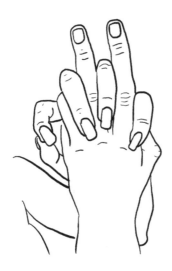

/we spent the whole day in bed
comparing his hand to mine
kissing my neck like I had just gotten back from war
feeling his fingers run up and down my curves
laughing in his arms
I felt safe here\

/you like what you like
it's difficult to change what we're drawn to\

/even though I'd known him for four years
I never seemed to get bored of him
I didn't need caffeine when I was around him
he was the fire which ignited my spirit\

/I caught my storytelling abilities from my mom
she projects with such enthusiasm and animation\

/the ego is the enemy\

/I remember how she said,
being an artist,
is it a curse?
or a blessing?\

/somewhere in paradise the wolves talk

he kept me feeling oh so intimate
while parading me in golden showers

put me on your record player
'n let it spin

less talk for a while
over Three Floyd's and Modelo's
let your sorrow fizz to the bottom of the barrel

made love on the kitchen counter
carried me up three flights of stairs after cooking for twelve hours

knows when to jump in
he said my p*ssy tastes like mangos and cinnamon
whilst those lame ass guys who can't hit
they play me a tune on the worlds tiniest violin

maybe I've been too rough with a more delicate man

down, down deep to my roots
how my Arabic ancestors hate to lose
bleeding within indigos and violet hues

knowing he's already lost so much
nobody truly knows the pain he's undergone
smoldered in marijuana clouds now
hope he can come back down

I suppose, I have been too rough
with a more delicate man.\
/only 20 percent of women get orgasms from just penetration
I was the lucky 20 percent
I guess\

BLOOD ORANGE

/I remember
how Lil Bit told me,
now I know
you aren't as innocent as you like

/if we treated every day
as an opportunity to improve our enlightenment
of the world
and of ourselves
we could obtain so much more knowledge\

/I am proud of the woman I am becoming
being held captive in the dark for so long
when I emerged into the light I've never glowed so bright\

/why aren't we more happy
for other peoples success?
why don't we use that as motivation

to be better?
while still being happy for them\

/I have some sexual tension with my ideal career\

/there is something about going out to breakfast
with your best friends
to sip on some warm coffee
and chat about last nights affairs\

/I wasn't sure how this would end
or how this would begin with him
but I knew it would be different
than last time\

/it's very convenient
having my neighbor
be my friends with benefits\

/I love making food for people
and watching them fall in love with the flavors\

/when you're cooking
it's all about the flavors
you have to have your acid
your fat
your salt
your protein
your spice
your sweet
your starch\

/cooking is one of my love languages\

/we hold so much ability
power in our words
strength in women
a sharp tongue holds the verse
don't linger too long on past guilt
my past shame weighs me down
so low
up until I let go
I let go
nostalgia runs me cold
through my veins of violet blood stains
the girl with the violet eyes talks of the swallows of Capistrano
as she leans out her window
she told me to come back
that leaving this place would bring me peace
to let go and follow the swallows all the way to Capistrano
in turn
I'll go

I met my twin flame again
in my dreams last night
haven't heard from him in so long
good to see my old friend before dawn

he knows I hold resentment
although he continues to sweet talk me back to sleep
as if nothing ever happened

goodbye twin
seems to vanish in the flames
left the both of us in pain
he reappears here
in my dreams
when I am at my most vulnerable state
goodbye twin flame\

/I rolled over
to be welcomed by him
and I felt better
that I was waking up next to him\

/young people
VOTE
you have power in your voice
they try to silence us because they assume we're young and naive
but our voice matters
we're louder if we stand together
we're louder if we go vote
pay attention to who we elect into office
pay attention to your local voting polls

please
as young people we need to be heard too\

/people want to talk about book smarts
but what about street smarts?
I can't stand a b*tch who can't read the room\

/there are no easy friends with benefits
when we both simmered with feelings\

/he told me
if you put your hand in a jar
and picked out somebody else's problem in exchange for yours
you'd realize that yours isn't as bad
as the rest of the jar\

/I beg of men
to be more vocal about rape
of sexual assault
this does not just involve women speaking out

we need our brothers here to fight along side us
rape culture is too common
3 out of five women have experienced sexual assault of some kind
    in their lives
please don't let our women suffer alone
we need our brothers here too\

/manifesting destiny
starts with cherishing your desires
it starts with positive affirmations
belief and hope
it begins with action and motivation
it rules with growing and expanding your horizons
but believing in yourself
really, truly believing in yourself
is the only way you can manifest your own destiny\

/I found that I needed to stop
comparing my old tragedies
to new beginnings\

/you got me brain dazed
fantasizing
not hiding
the way I am feeling
about you baby
love cushion me with your warm kiss\

/Chicago makes it hard to trust people
a lot of these Chicagoans
wonder what they gain and take from you\

/my talent is not based on the price you're willing to pay\

working with musicians-

/I may not say something out loud
but you bet I'm keeping tabs in my notes
don't cross the line
you'll be toast

when a man tries to over use me
I go ghost
gotta wait for this bitch
before he gets the roast
no this ain't a joke
this ain't no hoax
are you broke?
I'm not your price tag
I'm your boss
you're on my budget boy
get lost
'cause you cant mansplain me
you're lost
of what you lost
and what you've gained
I'm not your main creative to overuse and get played\

/I've found that if you do things out of pure love
for your art
and good intentions to inspire hope in others
money and fame will follow\

/my father would always tell me,
don't do it for the money
do it for the love of your art\

/we're not above nature
we are
one with nature\

/everything you're going through
is God preparing you
for something stronger\

/this is not permanent
everything is temporary\

/I talk too much when I'm passionate\

/I looked at myself in the mirror
hugging my curves
sometimes
you just want someone to love\

/think about the energy that you attract\

/magic is love
and energy\

/I kept him by my side
going to Church
with my vintage Gucci purse
pray the lord forgives me for my sins
looking for the lord
calling for the loud
smoking that flower
praise the father
give these seeds to the mother
so she can make a garden out of another\

/when you do a job
do it to the best of your abilities
everything you do reflects onto
you\

/know your worth
and add tax to that\

/I was sure this time around\

/be with someone
who knows what ambition feels like\

/he knew so much about me
yet every day felt so new when I was with him\

/as you hold me
I feel strong and powerful
beauty doused
of violets in your mouth
from this back porch
we sit on the ledge
to watch the sunset
keeping this consistent
I've been waitin'
yearning for your affection
had I noticed
I'd forgotten how close this is
to dive into your heart
to mix yellow into violet
blood orange all over the carpet
made love on the counter
blood orange in the refrigerator
blood orange on my record player
you spin me like the vinyl on your daddy's mantel
leave me out to wonder
I want to linger on your mind a bit longer
wish you were here
call me when he's working late
calls me when he's running late
find myself missing you the next day\

/he showered me in love and affection
he'd stop me for a second
just to admire my beauty
touch my olive skin like an oil painting
he told me of how lucky he was
to be able to hold me\

/all those years ago
how toxic we were
like gorilla glue to raw skin
I felt him sinking in
again
things change
when people grow out of toxic traits\

/he was hard
not to love\

/the girl with the violet eyes called me,
she asked me if being beautiful
was a curse
or a blessing\

BLOOD ORANGE

/I need to work on being more patient\

/you have to live in this body
so you might as well love it\

/if he wants someone else
I'll let him go
I would not fight to keep him in my arms
I will not compete for his attention
I will not be jealous of other women
I am not the one to put him in a secure box
to secure my insecurities of making sure he does not cheat on me
if he wants to cheat he will
there is no stopping a wild dog from that rabbit
no matter how much of a leash you have on that mutt
if he is determined he'll run

I would rather not work so hard
to keep an unwanted man
in my already warm arms
he should be just fine here\

/support your friends
play their music in the car
shout them out on social media
buy their work
why are we so quick to repost Kylie Jenner
and not our friends?\

/I envied the girl with the violet eyes
when she was only human too\

/and it rained and rained
for several days
yet numbing the silence with work and him\

/because my heart sank
in a whole different way
when I got that call
the girl with the violet eyes was in the hospital\

15. the woman with the violet eyes

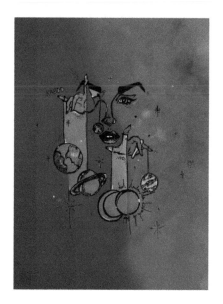

everyone loved her eyes–

/he loved her so much
you could see without looking that he saw nobody else
and it was like nature to him
he grew to her

wanted her when she rained
needed her light
and when she woke up
he was always there before school
waiting outside on her porch
carrying in McDonalds to pick her up
without knowing how much everyone else could see
that he loved her so much without even recognizing how much he
    loved her
and yet she saw right through him
and I remember seeing that
my whole life
him quietly love her
yet how loud his love was
and she had the ability to tune him out
like a switch on her car radio
turn him back on
when she wanted some
it bothered me
though I never told anyone
how I would've killed to have a man like that
to even love me just enough
to be infatuated by every little thing she voiced
her annoying habits
he loved those as well
I have never said that I did
but I have always wanted that
to be loved for who I am
I wanted someone to love me

the whole me
not to only desire me
not to want me for some nights when he's lonely
not to want me as a side piece
not to only find me thrilling when he's bored with other girls or
    tired of his homies
I am worn out from men finding me intriguing
that leaves them wondering of who I am
and I want him to know the whole me
really know me
I want him to go to bed with me
share a blunt with me
wake up next to me
not with anybody else
and I don't want him to think he needs to reassure me
I don't want him to have to say out loud
I want us both to feel this
only for us to say to ourselves,
how I love this fucking person

\remember
nobody else
can do it like you,
she told me\

/*nobody else could be you,*
I said to her\

/from a car accident
back in Minnesota
on the highway
going to Mendota
too far from where I was
the girl with the violet eyes was paralyzed\

/I remember in that moment
I wanted to take on her pain
be her sell sword
fight for her
my friend should not go through this alone\

/*who's going to want me now?*
she cried out to me
someone,
there will be someone out there

who'll love you,
I emphasized\

/I spent days on the phone with her
crying
trying
to make her laugh
booking my flight
to Minnesota
she needed me
as I needed her
all these years
now it was my turn
to be strong
though I knew facing her would be fatal\

/getting on that airplane
I buried my face in my hands
crying cold tears
for my friend\

/*I'll be in a wheel chair
for the rest of my life,*
she said to me
and I really did not know how to console her
it felt out of my control
yet she was so beautiful
dazzling with brilliance and light
though hers had faded somewhat
and I didn't blame her\

For her-

/I saw the morning sun in her face
and for the first time
she covered her violet eyes
turning towards me
she whispered weakly,
Carmen, pray for me,
while I thought to myself that I wasn't any good at prayer
or that I didn't believe much in religion
or that I was not sure of what to believe in
but as her illuminating eyes reflected mine
I saw for the first time
the darkest shade of violet

it was as if death came knocking on my door
with champagne and cigarettes
to tell me
of my friends dying wish

that nothing more
was left in her
besides a miracle
the pain was wilting away at her exterior
pray for me,
she said again
I wasn't confident in how powerful that my prayer could fix her
especially coming from this cynic
I know you don't pray, but believe in this one

I woke up every morning since
and I prayed
pleading to the world
beginning to the universe
for more time
for her
to whomever would listen
I prayed my heart out
for
her\

/we're either pawns or queens,
I told her
as I handed that chess piece back to her\

/she looked up at me with her violet eyes
pawns or queens...
she murmured,
smoothing out the crown with her fingers
queens,
I said\

/*what's new?*
she asked me
while I wheeled her around the hospital
I'm seeing the neighbor again,
I muttered
really? I knew it\

/*will you stay here?*
she asked me subtly

yes,
I said
I slept over at the hospital
with *Sex and The City* reruns on
I left to get her pancakes and bacon from Mickey's Diner
we cried and laughed and cried some more\

/ *who in their heart*
is going to love a cripple?
she said cynically
I do,
I told her\

/I learned
to not take anything in life for granted
I am trying to be more appreciative for what I have
because it could change in an instant\

/tell yourself
that these tragedies will become my art
repeat after me:
these tragedies will become my art

/the only way out
is through,
she said to me\

/if you give up on your passions
you're giving up on yourself\

/there are two of the most important days
the day you were brought into this world
and the day you discovered why\

/I want you to think of your life

a year ago
what did you obtain since then?
what hurt you back then
are you friends still the same?
what have you eliminated from your life?
and what have you gained?

where do you want to be a year from now?\

/after two weeks in Minnesota
I came back home
I was greeted with work
and him
it was so nice to feel him again\

/your smile
lights me on fire
it is so warm here
as your eyes watch mine
I get nervous
when I feel your skin
your chest and muscles
I dive in
warm in these arms
my body feels safe in yours
when you ask about me
when you care for me
when you fight for me
my heart smiles
thank you for being there
when nobody else was\

/learning how to manage my suffering anxiety and suffocating de-
    pression has been my biggest struggle and my most rewarding
    success\

/do not forget your friends
when you're with a man

find balance\

/*what is love feel like to you?*
the girl with the violet eyes asked subtly
love is like
coming home,
after you've been drenched in the rain\

/counting the roses I've thrown over balconies
I want to lounge around on your throne in your fantasies
I'll stay here
don't you worry
keep you in good company
letting the lingerie make me
I'll be throwing roses over balconies
I'll see you in my wet dreams\

/I'm turning into a girly girl
where my tomboys at?\

/I remember the only times I've felt utterly broken
and unfixable
I broke down in a mental panic
the only times I've felt comfortable in asking for help
was from my best friend, Erin
and my mom
they were the only two whom I really allowed to see me break\

/our mental health can kill us quietly
more than our physical health
remember that your mental health is a muscle you need to work
    out and flex too\

/dealing with
PTSD
flash backs of trauma
sleep paralysis
vivid dreaming
panic attacks
deepening depression
body dysmorphia
paranoia
suffocating anxiety
delusional episodes

all of this, is a colossal mess sometimes
and it breeds fear in us more often than anything else
I find that writing it down and saying it out loud helps
welcoming it to the forefront of your reality
getting comfortable with what makes us uncomfortable
reminding yourself what purpose you serve
and you do serve a purpose
every morning telling yourself that you are in control
to be sitting in the drivers seat is a choice, otherwise life will drive
     you\

/I thanked my parents
for lending me their armor
I thanked the girl with the violet eyes
for showing me friendship even from so far away
I thanked my neighbor
for being my best friend and my most brave fighter
I thanked my coworkers
for showing me the determination I needed to become a better
     person
I thanked my friends
for being one of my biggest supporters
and most trustworthy companions
I thanked my enemies
for being worthy appoints

who do you thank?\

/I am all in one
and still learning\

/after a while
I made sense of my tragedies\

/don't hesitate on holding your truth
even with the things that are hard to accept
or the things we hide
know that it is apart of you
embrace your truth
you don't have to explain it to anybody else
besides yourself\

/karma will catch your enemies too
I promise\

/I am so blessed
to have fallen in love
with my best friend
though it took a minute
at the beginning it was toxic
fell into the wrong pocket
shouldn't have done it
but we've come so far
now it feels right
I know things are aligned now\

/I've come to realize
that it is not a character flaw of mine
to be so loyal
it's not my fault I am loyal
it's their fault that they aren't\

/I've accepted my truth
now
you do the same\

/I've found
that I don't have to be alone
to be a free spirit\

/I was so envious of her
everything seemed to shine
like glitter
so beautiful
that the flowers grew for her
so wise the masters sang for her
the cranes bowed for her
she is still so beautiful now
she just has to find that love that I see
in herself\

/that's the thing in life
an everyday
reoccurrence
to love ourselves
to live for ourselves first
there is so much in you
that deserves to be loved

in the right way
you deserve authentic love\

/keep me in the moment
love me til I am myself again,
she whispered\

/don't feed the fear,
I said to her\

/I'll go on that date
if you finish the book you've been writing,
she told me
the first time we hung out since fall started
I went back to Minnesota for a little while
to see her and my family
the wind was cold and crisp
blood orange spilt
when you can walk again,
I said

if I walk again,
she murmured
you will walk again,
I told her\

/*this guy in my emotional support group said to me,*
"have you seen Forest Gump?"
"'cause you remind me of Lieutenant Dan",
the girl with the violet eyes busted out laughing
that's horrible,
I smirked a little\

/when I finally came home
he met me down at the boulevard
embraced me in his arms
crying
because life is so hard
though I am very blessed
I want to shower the world
with love and happiness
I am reminded
it's an everyday challenge to be met\

/as hard as it is
I love being a woman\

to you I write-

/we went down different paths
that were paved side by side
when the willow trees grow heavy and strong
and when the branches sway too low to the ground
know that I am somewhere near
I will see you again at the end of our roads\

/ what's more important?
she asked,
tracing her finger on my veined hands
holding on...
or letting go?

CPSIA information can be obtained
at www.ICGtesting.com
Printed in the USA
LVHW021823081220
673652LV00011B/23